DEMOCRACY
AND ACCOUNTABILITY
IN THE LABOUR PARTY

Democracy and Accountability in the Labour Party

Edited by John B. Burnell

Spokesman
for the Institute for Workers' Control

First published in 1980 by Spokesman, for the Institute for Workers' Control, Bertrand Russell House, Gamble Street, Nottingham NG7 4ET

Cloth ISBN 0 85124 299 5
Paper ISBN 0 85124 300 2

Printed by the Russell Press Ltd., Nottingham

Contents

Preface   7

Introduction   9

Summary and Main Proposals
1. Reforming the Parliamentary Labour Party   14
      The Need for Reform
      Proposals for Reform
2. Election of the Party Leadership: In support of
   an Electoral College   19
3. The Selection and Reselection of Parliamentary
   Candidates   22
      Who Should Select the Parliamentary Candidate
      Improvements to the Selection Procedure
4. The National Executive Committee   26
      Its Role and Authority
      The Composition of the NEC
5. Reforming Annual Conference   31
      The Balance of Voting Power at Annual Conference
      Improvements to Conference Procedure
       i. Improving Policy Making
       ii. Conference, the PLP and the NEC
      iii. Making Conference Procedures More Democratic
6. Party Membership   41
7. Local Government Democracy   43

Background Papers
1. Parliamentary Candidates   47
2. The National Executive Committee   57
A Note of Dissent from the Proposal for "Joint Control"   86

Preface

The Party Structure Group, whose members are listed below, has been meeting since early in 1978. The Group was established largely as a result of the belief that there was a need for a forum for discussion on Party reform, and that the Group could provide such a forum.

The decision of the 1979 Conference to set up the Enquiry gave added impetus to the Group's discussions. Whilst not the only outlet for our ideas, clearly the Enquiry provided a focus for our attention, and the proposals contained in this booklet have been submitted to the Enquiry.

Papers on each topic were written by individual members of the Group, which then discussed them in some detail. These have been consolidated after extensive debate, and some are published here as background papers. Inevitably the separate papers reflect the particular approach of their authors. Some disagreements, however, were left unrecorded as for the most part they concerned specific proposals to which some members believed they had better alternatives.

The *Summary and Main Proposals* section, on the other hand, expresses views with which all members of the Group were in broad agreement, and this has formed the main part of our submission to the Party Enquiry. With one proposal, however, relating to the views expressed in the section *The Role, Authority and Composition of the NEC*, some members of the Group were in fundamental disagreement. (See Note of Dissent, p.86.)

The Group has no formal status, and no constitution. All its members serve in a personal capacity, and hope to continue their discussions on an occasional basis after the Party Enquiry has reported.

We are grateful to the IWC for their assistance in the publication of this booklet, and stress that the views contained in it are not necessarily those of the IWC. We are glad to be afforded this opportunity to further in a small way the efforts to ensure that Labour Governments implement Labour Party policies.

Reg Race (Chairman)

Members of the Group contributing to this booklet are:
Hilary Benn (Secretary)
John Burnell
Ken Coates
Vladimir Derer
Michael Meacher
Frances Morrell
Reg Race (Chairman)
Pat Seyd
Eric Shaw
Barrie Sherman
Stuart Weir
Pete Willsman

Introduction

It is commonplace to argue that the Labour Party constitution is outmoded and needs replacing by structures and processes which are more up-to-date. This is not a new theory; but in advancing it we must remember that the 1918 constitution, drafted largely by Sidney and Beatrice Webb, had purposes other than the obvious ones of giving the Labour Party a more formal socialist ideology and the device of individual membership. Richard Crossman identified these hidden purposes and objectives in his introduction to the 1963 edition of Walter Bagehot's book *The English Constitution.*

"In order to break down the walls of social oligarchy which surrounded Parliament, a battering ram was required, and the Labour Party was created for this purpose. Its structure was determined by three conditions. First, it must have very large funds at its disposal; hence the reliance on trade union financing which led to the sponsoring of trade union candidates by particular unions. Secondly, since it could not afford, like its opponents, to maintain a large army of paid party workers, the Labour Party required militants — politically conscious socialists to do the work of organising the constituencies. But since these militants tended to be 'extremists', a constitution was needed which maintained their enthusiasm by apparently creating a full party democracy while excluding them from effective power. Hence the concession in principle of sovereign powers to the delegates at the annual conference, and the removal in practice of most of this sovereignty through the trade union block vote on the one hand, and the complete independence of the Parliamentary Labour Party on the other."

This crisp and perceptive analysis of the Labour Party's constitution and the effective structure of power within the party which it created is increasingly shared by thousands of party members, especially following the failures of the 1964-70 and

9

1974-79 Labour Governments to implement party policy and to engineer a "fundamental shift of wealth and power in favour of working people and their families".

Indeed, the performance of the last Labour Government in relation to the manifesto promises made in February 1974, and in relation to the content of the 1973 party programme, has created an atmosphere in which serious-minded party members are searching for ways of ensuring that such problems do not occur again.

The last Labour Government deliberately sabotaged the party's industrial strategy by imposing considerable restraints on the powers of the National Enterprise Board by restricting the finance available to it, by destroying the credibility of planning agreements by making them voluntary, and by imposing only a ramshackle co-ordination of industry plans through the sector working parties of the National Economic Development Council. In addition the Government introduced major cuts in public spending in 1975 and early 1976, and later in 1976 acceded to the demands of the International Monetary Fund by agreeing to a permanent reduction in the share of Gross Domestic Product taken by public expenditure, and by specific and damaging cuts in a wide range of spending programmes. The Government also abandoned any pretence of maintaining full employment, and budgeted for near zero rates of economic growth; thus, in commenting on the 1977 Budget, the right-wing journal the *Economist* said: "This Budget aims at nearly the lowest growth and risks nearly the worst rise in unemployment in all 36 fiscal years since Keynesian budgets in Britain began". The Social Contract was transformed, in the eyes of trade unionists, from an agreement about economic and social priorities into a vehicle for implementing a policy of wage restraint — culminating in the stubborn determination of the Cabinet in seeking to impose the 5% pay policy on the trade union movement, against the advice of Congress and the Labour Party Conference. These attacks on specific manifesto commitments and the Party Programme have created a new political situation in the party, in which activists are demanding the introduction of democracy and accountability; for, if accountability had been in operation during the lifetime of the last Labour Government, then the end result might have been considerably different.

If we examine the political record of the last ten years, it is clear that the activists and the party conference have been correct on a number of important issues, and the parliamentary leadership wrong. Vietnam, cuts in public expenditure, and the 5% pay policy are examples.

However, the Group does not regard the democratic changes proposed in this report as being sufficient conditions for the successful implementation of socialist party policies. There will also have to be substantial ideological changes in the PLP and elsewhere in the Labour Movement if success is to be achieved.

There is, of course, an important external reason underlining the necessity for radical changes in democratic accountability in the Labour Party. This is the advent of the Thatcher government and its attendant full-blooded monetarist policies, reflected in their determination to destroy the political and social settlement of 1945 and with it the compromise of the mixed economy. Their attempt to reintroduce market forces into areas previously in the public sector, their policies of deflation and restriction of the powers of organised labour through increased unemployment and changes in the laws affecting trade unions, require an urgent political response from the Labour Party. That response will only be credible if it contains substantial improvements in the accountability of the next Labour Government to the wider Labour Movement, and whereby a Labour cabinet will be committed firmly to the introduction of the policies agreed by the Party. Without such changes in accountability, it is likely that a future Labour administration will accept some critical aspects of current Conservative Government policy, and that these Tory policies will form the cornerstones of a permanent political and social settlement.

The urgent need for democracy and accountability is underlined by the relative political decline of the Labour Party as a mass organisation. The party now enjoys its lowest share of the popular vote in general elections since 1935; the individual membership of the party declined disastrously during the 1964-70 Labour Government, and has only since been stabilised; and it is now widely accepted that in many constituencies the Labour Party is nothing more than an electoral machine, and an inefficient one at that. This fossilisation of the party as an organisation is partly the product of the economic crisis, in which Labour

Governments have often been seen by the City of London and informed management as the government most likely to persuade working people to contain their economic, social and political demands, and in which Labour Governments have sometimes acted in this way — to the confusion of their supporters amongst working people. It is also the product of a situation in which the Labour Party has, for most of its political life, been immune from competition for the votes of the working class. Unlike most continental Socialist parties, the Labour Party has never had to vie with a mass Communist Party or with other serious groupings on the Left for the electoral support of working people; and this lack of ideological competition has resulted in a serious arteriosclerosis of Labour's ideology and organisation.

These developments and circumstances have completely undermined the right-wing view of the Labour Party organisation as a method simply of garnering votes and securing the election of Labour councillors and Members of Parliament to public bodies. The internal structure, processes and organisation of the Labour Party are now seen by a majority of Party activists as crucial to the implementation of socialist policies. In short, the Labour Party is currently undergoing a radicalisation of its policies, leadership and organisation similar to those periods of radicalisation which have taken place at earlier stages in the party's history.

The changes that are required in the internal structure of the Party must also recognise that two majority groups in the population are effectively discriminated against inside the apparatus of the Party itself. Working people — and particularly manual workers — are under-represented on many key party committees, on many local authority Labour Groups, and in Parliament. The position of women inside the Party is even more ludicrous; they are relegated in many local parties to the role of tea makers and sandwich cutters; they are even more grossly under-represented on local authorities, in Parliament, and in the Party generally; and the leadership of the Party has ignored the growth of the women's movement in Britain — one of the most significant political events of the last generation — in what can only be described as a reckless fashion. The Group felt that there was a need for positive discrimination in favour of women in almost all the party institutions discussed: the PLP, NEC, and

NEC sub-committees remain dominated by men. There was disagreement, however, on how far the Party should go in providing for this positive discrimination in its institutions. We all agreed, for example, that seats on the NEC should be provided for women members; but some members of the Group wanted to go considerably further than this: for example, a target quota of fifty per cent of the places on Parliamentary shortlists, and on the NEC and its sub-committees, was proposed.

The Party Structure Group believes that the proposals set out in this booklet are vitally necessary, germane to the social, political and economic problems facing the Party at this crucial stage in its history, and important to the success of the next Labour Government. We hope that the specific proposals set out by the Group will commend themselves to the movement and will contribute to the important discussions on party structure following the report of the Commission of Inquiry and thereafter.

Reforming the Parliamentary Labour Party

The Need for Reform

The PLP betrays little awareness that its role is to represent the aspirations and needs of working people with proudly different political traditions, as opposed to the interests represented by the other parties. Rather, the majority of the PLP anxiously conforms to the conventions and styles set by the establishment parties. Most Labour MPs appear to have the same conception of their role as do Tory and Liberal MPs. They see themselves as representatives very much as defined by Burke: they claim the right to exercise their individual judgement, and on that basis to treat the Party's Election Manifesto and Programme as little more than advisory.

Paradoxically, Labour MPs have virtually no opportunities to make independent decisions, unless they are Cabinet or Shadow Cabinet Ministers. When Labour is in office, real power lies with Whitehall and the Cabinet, its exercise protected by the Official Secrets Act. Labour MPs, far from exercising independent judgement, are whipped through the Lobbies in support of policy decisions about which they have scarcely been informed, much less consulted.

In considering the PLP, the Group identified the following main shortcomings in its role and organisation at present:

a. a direct relationship of genuine accountability to Party Conference has not been established.

b. it has no real powers of accountability over its leaders when the Party is in office and its leaders are in senior Ministerial positions.

c. it is not seriously consulted by its leaders in advance of major decisions being taken, or important Bills promulgated, while in government.

d. the machinery for making the PLP into a forum for democratic

14

decision-making is not being operated, i.e. there are relatively few debates on major issues, and almost none which lead to a decision by vote which is then binding on the Party's leaders.

e. it is not effectively integrated into the wider structure of the Party throughout the country because no minutes of its proceedings are circulated to Members, let alone to CLPs, and even more importantly no record of decisions taken, including the distribution of Members' voting, is available (except to the Shadow Cabinet).

f. it has not established a complementary role and working relationship with the NEC whereby their respective dual roles of accountability can be operated with reasonable harmony and compatibility.

Proposals for Reform

These proposals should be considered together with the section on the power and authority of the NEC, and in conjunction with the proposals for joint control outlined later. For example, proposals for legislation would first be agreed with the PLP — but would then require the subsequent agreement of the NEC before being put foward to Parliament.

a. In common with the principle of accountability which has now been adopted for MPs, the PLP should have the right, in the course of the normal 5 year Parliamentary term, to elect and re-select the Cabinet when the Party is in government. (The election and re-selection of the Leader and Deputy Leader of the PLP is dealt with in a separate section.) There are already annual elections for the Parliamentary Committee (although we feel that its size should be increased to 24) and it seems perverse that this procedure should be wholly abandoned at precisely the time when accountability by election really matters, i.e. when the leaders of the Party are wielding executive power in command of the departments of State. The PLP should therefore institute a procedure when the Party is in office for the election and re-selection (say, every 2 years) of all members of the Cabinet. This process would start with the election of the Cabinet at the beginning of the lifetime of each Labour Government, and it would be combined with the election of all front bench spokesmen in opposition. In our

15

view, at least the four most important posts (i.e. Chancellor of the Exchequer, Foreign Secretary, Home Secretary and Leader of the House) should be individually elected. It is accepted that there needs to be a degree of flexibility over these elections, leaving the Leader with the right to supplement them by appointments where necessary to posts requiring particular qualifications, e.g. the Scottish Office, the Welsh Office, and the Law Officers' Department.

b. At present the lack of consultation with the PLP before the presentation of Bills or the introduction of significant new policy proposals, together with the subsequent operation of the whipping system, has effectively neutered the role of the back benches when the Party is in government. In order to resuscitate this role, the following new procedures should be instituted:

i. the draft of the Queen's Speech should be first presented to the PLP long enough before presentation to Parliament so that, in the light of back bench comments, amendments can be made, omissions avoided, and the draft voted on.

ii. the outline draft of all Bills and other major policy proposals should be brought before the PLP first for consultation, amendment and voting on prior to publication. The most important Bills or other proposals should come before the full PLP, and less important ones should be brought to the relevant back bench committee.

iii. in general the PLP subject groups should be allotted a much more significant consultative role, and in particular the appointment of front bench spokesmen to speak for the Party should be subject to their recommendation. They should also have the right to nominate members for Committees of the House in their own policy area, and generally should be consulted and have their views taken into account on all major policy initiatives in their own area. On the other hand, it is accepted that the responsibilities of the subject groups need to be taken more seriously than in the past, and in particular that the election of chairmen, to prevent abuses that have sometimes previously occurred, should be restricted to among those with at least a minimum reasonable attendance record in the previous year.

c. The PLP should be treated seriously (which it is not at the moment) as a forum for the taking of important decisions in a democratic manner. This requires several changes both of procedure and attitude:

    i. The meetings of the PLP should decide by vote all matters concerning the work of the PLP (including whipping, appointments, visits, etc.), subject to the over-riding authority of Conference.

    ii. Minutes of PLP proceedings should not simply be kept privately, as at present, but circulated as a matter of routine to all Members.

    iii. Votes on key issues should be recorded, and the lists of those voting for and against should be circulated with the minutes of meetings. For at present it is certainly anomalous that whipped votes in the Chamber are recorded in detail in Hansard, but open votes in the PLP on equally important decisions are not recorded.

d. The decision-making role of the PLP needs to be much more clearly understood within the Party outside as a whole. This too requires new or changed procedures:

    i. The standing orders of the PLP, which should be laid before Conference for approval, should contain explicit recognition that it is the first duty of the PLP to implement Party policy, as contained in both the Manifesto and the decisions of Annual Conference. Also, the acceptance form for Parliamentary condidates should contain a clear reference to the candidates' duty to seek to implement the policies of the Party.

    ii. The PLP office should make available the voting records of Members, both in the House and in PLP meetings, to all CLPs on a regular basis.

    iii. Minutes of PLP meetings should also be regularly circulated to all CLPs.

e. It is imperative that a better and closer working relationship be established between the PLP and the NEC in a manner which properly safeguards the respective roles of each. Amongst the most important changes that need to be considered are:

    i. When the Party is in government, there ought to be consultation *before* decisions are taken rather than merely ratification after the event. What is therefore needed is a special joint NEC-Cabinet committee to meet weekly just before the Cabinet, to discuss items due to be considered by the Cabinet and any other issues outstanding at the time, on the understanding that proposals which are not broadly agreed should be referred back for further consideration. At least one Member specifically representing back bench interests should be included on this joint committee.

ii. On the basis of these regular joint meetings, the NEC should prepare a report on the PLP's activities over the course of the previous year for presentation to Conference, and the PLP should have the right to comment on this report.

f. A relationship of genuine accountability to the Party Conference needs to be built on the following procedural innovation:

i. The NEC-PLP report to Conference on the PLP's activities in the past year should form the basis for a half-day debate at Conference following the Leader's speech, and future PLP activities should be guided by the views of Conference.

Election of the Party Leadership

In support of an electoral college

In looking at the way in which the Leader and Deputy Leader of the Party are elected, the Group was guided by the three principles which it has sought to apply to all its deliberations; namely, greater accountability, wider democracy and more openess.

At the moment the election of the Leader is done on a completely unrepresentative basis. MPs, and only MPs, are involved. As a result, even when the Party has a majority in the House of Commons, hundreds of constituency parties are prevented from even having an indirect say in the choice of the Leader, and those CLPs with MPs are hardly better off as they cannot mandate their MPs and have no way of knowing how they have voted. In addition, affiliated trade unions are completely excluded from the process.

The Group agreed to support the establishment of an electoral college for the purpose of electing the Leader and Deputy Leader of the Party, on which fair representation would be given to all those in the Party with a clear and direct interest: the trade unions, CLPs, MPs (and possibly endorsed Parliamentary candidates). Such a college would be truly representative of the Party, and it would make the Leader and Deputy Leader accountable to the movement as a whole. The process of election would also be open, with delegates casting their votes in accordance with their mandates (in the case of trade union and constituency delegates) or their own publicly expressed views (in the case of MPs and candidates). A further argument in favour of this change is that the practice of electing Parliamentary leaders by a wider constituency is common among the Socialist parties of Europe where it has worked successfully.

As to the composition of the electoral college, the Group recognised that there were different ways of constructing it.

One model is that advocated by the Campaign for Labour Party Democracy, which would consist of:

i. all Labour Members of Parliament;
ii. all endorsed prospective Parliamentary candidates;
iii. one Annual Conference delegate from each Constituency Labour Party. Delegates of Constituency Labour Parties which had not as yet chosen a prospective Parliamentary candidate would have two votes each;
iv. delegates from affiliated organisations other than Constituency Labour Parties who would have a total number of votes double that of affiliated Constituency Labour Parties; these votes being divided in proportion to their affiliated members, with each affiliated organisation having at least one vote.

Another model would have voting strength divided as follows:

Trade Unions	40%
CLPs	40%
MPs	20%

This model provides for parity between the unions and the CLPs.

The Group did not come down firmly in support of one particular model, but were in agreement that certain procedures should be followed in the operation of an electoral college (of whatever composition), and these are listed below.

i. All votes cast in the election of the Party Leader and Deputy Party Leader would be recorded and this information made available to all affiliated organisations.
ii. When the Party is in opposition the Leader and Deputy Leader would be nominated and elected annually by exhaustive ballot by the college meeting at Annual Conference. Every affiliated organisation would be able to nominate a person for the offices of Leader and Deputy Leader, but the persons so nominated would have to be MPs.
iii. When the Party is in office, there would be one mandatory re-selection in each Parliament of the Leader and Deputy Leader by the college at Annual Conference between 18 and 36 months after the last election (with special provision for a further election by the college on request by any two of the following groups: a minimum of a third of the affiliated

organisations; the NEC; or a majority of the total membership of the PLP).

iv. If the Leader died or resigned at any time than a special meeting of Conference would be convened at which the College would operate to elect a successor. Delegates to this special electoral conference would normally be those who were delegates to the Party's last Annual Conference, unless affiliated bodies made their own separate arrangements. If this event occurred after 1st July in any year, the election would be held over until the next Annual Conference, unless a general election was deemed to be imminent. In the meantime the Deputy Leader would become Acting Leader. If the Deputy Leader died or resigned at any time, then the Cabinet or the Shadow Cabinet (as appropriate) would elect an acting successor until a new Deputy Leader could be elected by the college at the next Annual Conference.

v. There would be a presumption on the Leader or Deputy Leader to retire (if they intended to do so) at such a time so as to allow the college to elect a successor at Annual Conference.

vi. Finally, we suggest that candidates for either post should be required to issue a political statement prior to the election, to make a speech to the College and to answer questions from the floor.

The Selection and Reselection of Parliamentary Candidates

Who should select the Parliamentary Candidate?

The Group considered this question carefully, and much of the discussion centred on whether the final selection of a Parliamentary Candidate should be widened to include all Party members. In the end, it was generally agreed that the arguments in favour of selection remaining in the hands of the General Committee strongly outweighed those which favoured changing the present system.

It was felt that the GC — with its elected, delegate composition, its regular contact with the MP, and its representation of trade union branches — was the only body able properly to monitor the MPs actions, and therefore was best placed to be responsible for re-selection. Accountability would only be meaningful if it involved a continuous monitoring process.

Moreover, it was noted that responsibility for all other major decisions by constituency parties lies quite properly with the General Committee; it would not be sensible to set up a new structure, separate from the normal procedures, to take this one particular decision, the selection of a Parliamentary candidate.

In supporting the GC as the final selection body, the Group did recognise that there are many improvements that can and ought to be made to the selection process and these are summarised below.

Improvements to the Selection Procedure

i. GCs should examine ways of increasing their membership so as to allow the maximum possible participation by active members.

ii. All closing dates for nominations should be published in *Labour Weekly*.

iii. Each potential nominee should be given a list of affiliated organisations and secretaries' addresses and telephone numbers.

iv. Nominees should be required to produce written political statements, to be circulated to all branches prior to selection meetings.

v. All nominees should submit sufficient curricular vitae to the CLP Secretary, giving full details of all offices held and for how long.

vi. A CLP involved in selecting a Parliamentary candidate should be entitled to contact prospective nominees' own CLPs for the purposes of obtaining factual information only, about those nominees' length of membership, offices held, etc., with the proviso that the nominees should be allowed to see the replies from their own CLPs and be able to comment on them before they are sent to the selecting CLP.

vii. Each affiliated organisation/branch making a nomination must have a selection conference.

viii. Both the branch selection meeting and the GC final selection meeting should try to combine individual interviews with panel discussions between nominees.

ix. Branches should be permitted to discuss the merits of the nominees before deciding whom to nominate, but this principle should not be extended to the final selection meeting.

x. The Executive Committee of the GC must invite all the nominees for interview before shortlisting.

xi. Shortlisting by the Executive Committee should be by a single ballot, i.e., single, first-past-the-post ballot, rather than by an exhaustive eliminating ballot, to reduce the opportunities for tactical voting. It should also be laid down that the members of the Executive Committee should not be compelled to use their full number of votes; at present it is not uncommon for them to be instructed to vote against their wishes so as to use up all their votes, despite this 'ruling' being quite unfounded.

xii. Branches and affiliated organisations should be allowed to call together jointly or separately shortlisted nominees to

23

interview them. It was the view of some members of the Group that branches and affiliated organisations should be able to mandate their delegates to the final selection conference, following such a meeting.

xiii. A CLP must always hold a bona fide selection conference with a representative shortlist of nominees, unless only one nominee offers himself or herself for nomination.

xiv. A copy of the NEC guidelines relating to the final selection meeting, which are currently available to Regional Organisers, should be given to members at the beginning of the selection procedure, and should be published in the NEC Report each year.

xv. The Group recognised that mandatory re-selection increased the potential for "flooding/packing" of final selection meetings, and it was felt that the current safeguards were not sufficient. We therefore propose that the rules should be altered so as to insist that a member of the GC should have had to attend at least three meetings of the GC in the previous twelve months prior to the final selection meeting. The position of new delegates, who might not be able to fulfil this requirement − for instance, if the selection process was initiated shortly after the Party's AGM − was discussed, but it was felt that for the rule to operate it would have to be strictly applied. In general, CLPs would not initiate the selection process shortly after the AGM.

xvi. Where as organisation is already affiliated and increases its affiliation, its vote (i.e. number of delegates) at the GC should remain based on its former affiliation for a period of one year − in line with CLP affiliations to the National Party and their vote at Conference. New affiliates to a CLP should be immediately entitled to play a full role in the GC, except in the event of a Parliamentary selection procedure, in which case they should be disbarred for one year.

xvii. The Group also recognised that abuses occur in respect of the payment of delegates' expenses. It was noted that in some CLPs it is traditional to pay delegates who have travel difficulties or loss of earnings problems, as a result of working on night shift, etc. It was agreed that in these circumstances CLPs should pay expenses. However, this was not the same as cases in which affiliated organisations pay the expenses of all their delegates. It was felt that this was not acceptable and that a rule preventing this should be formulated if it was practicable to do so.

xviii. As a condition of nomination as a Parliamentary candidate, an individual should provide an official signed declaration that he or she, if elected, will abide, by, and seek to implement, the policies of the Party as set out in the Manifesto and the Labour Programme supplemented by resolutions of Annual Conference.

xix. The majority of the Group also felt that all shortlists for Parliamentary selections should include at least one member of the two disadvantaged majority sections of the population — manual workers and women, unless no such applications are forthcoming; and that the EC in the absence of such nominations being made, should have the power to make the necessary additions to the shortlist from amongst those who had put their names forward for consideration.

The National Executive Committee

Its Role and Authority

The Group started from the premise that the role of the NEC was to provide the positive leadership of the Party, and we noted the attempts that had been made in recent years by the NEC to strengthen this leadership by means of impressing upon the Parliamentary party the need to adhere to Party policy, by attempting to associate and involve the TUC in policy development, and by taking a close interest in the formulation of policy vis-a-vis the Manifesto.

However, the Group also noted that certain negative trends in relation to the role of the NEC had emerged during the 1974-1979 Labour Government and these were summarised as follows:

a. The status of the NEC in the eyes of the Labour Cabinet had been that of a pressure group, rather than the voice of the Party.
b. There was a lack of involvement of the Cabinet and other Ministers in Party policy making.
c. There was a lack of involvement by the Party in Government decision-making, particularly in respect of advance consultation on new measures.
d. The procedure for drawing up the election Manifesto was wholly unsatisfactory.
e. There was a lack of consultation with Party members in the development and endorsement of NEC policy statements.
f. The close alliance between the Cabinet and the TUC was used to undermine the status of the NEC.

The Group examined a number of possible options for upgrading the authority and influence of the NEC, and in the end a majority of the Group came down in favour of a system of *joint control*; in other words, a continuing series of negotiations between the NEC and the Parliamentary Party on policy implementation which would be undertaken on the clear understanding that no action be taken by either side in the absence of joint agreement. Joint control would involve a major change in the way that Parliamentary democracy works, or is meant to work, in this country. In effect, it would mean the end of the present system of Cabinet Government, at least whilst Labour is in power. The Cabinet, for example, would cease to be responsible (even in theory) only to Parliament and would become instead accountable also to the Party: and all of the conventions and secrecy which go to support Cabinet Government — and which make it impossible for the Party in practice to help shape the policy and practice of Labour Governments — would have to be abandoned. Similarly, individual Ministers would be expected to answer not only to Parliament, the Cabinet, and the PM, but also to the Party. In short, the Cabinet, and all Labour Ministers, would be bound, by the Party Constitution, to govern the country in joint stewardship with the representatives of the Party.

The new system would work as follows:

i. A statutory *policy liaison committee* drawn equally from the NEC and Cabinet, would meet before each Cabinet. It would have before it the agenda and papers to be considered by the Cabinet (subject only to the limitations on secrecy — for example, on defence — accepted by Conference in the Party's current policy on information disclosure). Any agreements reached within this committee would be ad referendum to the Cabinet: but wherever Cabinet endorsement was not forthcoming, then no action would be taken pending further negotiations with the Party.

ii. At the commencement of each session of Parliament, the PM would informally consult with the NEC (or its officers, or the policy liaison committee) on proposals for inclusion in the Programme of Legislation (the Queen's Speech); following these consultations, the draft Speech would be laid before a joint meeting of the full NEC and Cabinet (or joint committees thereof) so that the actual text could be jointly agreed, line by line.

iii. Chairmen of Cabinet Committees would be expected to keep appropriate NEC members and Party officials informed on the progress of business − and to seek agreement with the NEC (or with the appropriate NEC committee) − without waiting for the issues to come before the full Cabinet. Disagreements would be referred to the policy liaison committee.

iv. No Government statement, no Bill, no Budget, and no major Government action would be made or issued before joint agreement had been reached with the NEC or appropriate NEC committee.

v. No Parliamentary alliances would be sought or made before joint agreement had been reached with the NEC. The same would apply to the use of any kind of referenda (including the questions to be put before the electorate), to the granting of honours and distinctions; to the timing of the General Election; etc., etc.

vi. Wherever appropriate − and especially where there was disagreement or lack of enthusiasm on the part of the Party − the Government would be entitled to publish its proposals in 'consultative' form, as a Green Paper, Consultation Paper, or whatever; but the reservations of the Party should also be noted in such documents.

vii. Government Ministers would be expected to play a major role in assisting the NEC in its development of Party policy: and this would include their active participation on the advisory sub-committees and study groups of the NEC. Any serious disagreements would be referred upwards to the "policy liaison committee" − and especially wherever the issue concerned the preparation of draft NEC statements.

The Group felt that these proposals represented the most effective way of giving the Party a real voice in the implementation of Party policy, although it was also recognised that effective sanctions against representatives who failed to support Party policy would also be needed.

The Composition of the NEC

In considering the principles upon which the composition and method of election of the NEC should be based, the Group felt that the following were of crucial importance:

a. The NEC should be an executive body which is effectively accountable to the Party.
b. The NEC should be fully representative of the Party's membership, in the sense of being elected by it and being answerable to it.
c. The NEC should reflect as accurately as practicable those political forces in the Party which provide its underlying strength, i.e. the trade unions and the CLPs.
d. The NEC should reflect, as far as practicable, the class, sex and ethnic make-up of the Party's membership.

The Group agreed that as a starting point for reform, we should aim for parity of direct representation on the NEC for the two main pillars of the Party — the CLPs and the trade unions. In fact, this is a theme which runs throughout our recommendations. A majority of the Group felt that the Women's Section should be abolished and the reserved seats transferred to the CLP (3) and trade union sections (3) (at the same time as increasing their total number from 5 to 6) while a minority argued strongly for the retention of this Section, and for it to be elected by the Labour Women's Conference. It was also agreed that members of the TUC General Council should be allowed to sit on the NEC.

On the question of NEC representation for the PLP, the Labour Party Regions and local government, the Group rejected this idea as it would contravene the principle of direct accountability of NEC members to Annual Conference, and because (in the case of the PLP and local government) it would create a special privileged position for a handful of Labour Party members merely because they had been chosen by the Party as elected representatives. However, the Group did feel that there was a case for allowing an observer from local government to attend NEC meetings.

The majority of the Group therefore proposed that the composition of the NEC be changed to that set out below.

Elected Members
  Trade Unions   15 seats
  — 12 ordinary seats   } elected by
  — 3 seats reserved for women   } trade unions

  CLPs   15 seats
  — 12 ordinary seats   } elected by
  — 3 seats reserved for women   } CLPs

Treasurer — elected by whole Conference   1 seat

YS (the Group could not agree whether this   1 seat
      post should be filled at Annual Conference
      or at YS Conference)

Women's Section — seats abolished

Leader and Deputy Leader   elected by new   2 seats
                                  electoral college

Socialist Organisations   elected as at present   1 seat

                                  Sub-total (voting)   35

Observers
  PLP — Chairman (instead of Chief Whip)   1 seat

  Labour Group in European Assembly —   1 seat
      Leader of Group (as at present)

  Party Staff — one representative (as at present)   1 seat

  Local Government — one representative elected by   1 seat
      Labour Groups on local authority associations.

                                  Sub-total (non-voting)   4

                                  TOTAL   39

These changes could be implemented with the minimum of
disruption, and would, in our view, put the NEC on a much
sounder democratic footing.

Reforming Annual Conference

The balance of voting power at Annual Conference

One of the Group's consistent aims has been to establish the principle of parity of representation between the CLPs and the trade unions — the twin pillars of the party.

We therefore looked closely at the balance of voting strength at Annual Conference, and there was general agreement that there should be an increase in the voting power of the CLPs, which at present is only one-tenth of that of the trade unions.

The prime purpose of this proposal is to encourage a large individual membership which is of major importance to a mass political party. The CLPs are being asked to attract these new members, to raise a great deal more money (even though they already contribute as much to the Party through local fund-raising as do the trade unions at national level) to maintain an efficient electoral and local party organisation, to work in the sphere of local government and to initiate activities which will ensure a high level of political understanding among members. Yet despite the demands made on them, the CLPs have negligible political weight. It is naive to expect that in a democratic society, political activists can be recruited in large numbers when, at the same time, they are denied any real say in policy determination. This is particularly so when the programme, on the basis of which they are being recruited, is more often than not quickly jettisoned once the Party is returned as *the* government. In these circumstances it is hardly surprising that only the politically most committed — plus a steadily diminishing band of deferential members — continue to put in arduous hours of work for the Party.

In theory the political wing of the Party is dominant. The trade union movement, having created the Labour Party, has always accepted that a large measure of independence of the political wing is essential if the Party is to speak credibly on behalf of the great majority of the nation. Having ensured for themselves a vital place in the Party structure, the trade unions have never attempted to exercise control over the political wing. The trouble therefore is *not* that trade unions have too much political influence. The problems of the Party derive from the fact that, in practice, the power of the political wing has become the almost exclusive monopoly of the Parliamentary Labour Party. The constituency section, which carries the major share in the work of maintaining the Party, has only a very minor share in its political decision making, and this is clearly evident in the current imbalance of voting strength at Conference.

The Party's present affiliated trade union membership is 6,351,000 (1979 figure), but it must be recognised that the bulk of this membership is inactive within the Party. Is it really fair, therefore, that this section of the Party should hold ten times as many votes as the CLPs, which contain a much higher proportion of active members and which are responsible for so much fund-raising and organisational work? While this imbalance remains, the influence on Conference decisions of individual CLPs is marginal and this does not encourage new members to join. To increase the voting strength of CLPs would be to give them a much more significant role in decision-making at Conference, and would encourage party members to consider their decisions seriously and responsibly when mandating their Conference delegate.

In view of the equal importance of the CLPs and of the trade unions to the Party in terms of organisation and financial contributions, the Group came to the conclusion that we should move towards a system of parity voting for Annual Conference (i.e. in which the CLPs and trade unions would have an equal number of votes). It was recognised that such a system would have to include an element of flexibility to accommodate changing membership strengths; indeed it was felt that CLPs should be positively encouraged to recruit new members in order to increase their voting power.

We therefore propose the following scheme for increasing the voting strength of CLPs at Annual Conference.

organisation		Number	Votes
Trade Unions		50	6,351,000
CLPs		548	654,000
Socialist Societies		8	36,000
Co-op		2	29,000
	Total	608	7,070,000

It is proposed that the voting strength of the CLPs be increased by a factor of 10, on the basis of actual membership. Under this scheme, the CLPs vote at Conference would then (using 1978 membership figures but the 1979/80 affiliation proposals) be as follows:

6 CLPs would cast		233,000 votes
(i.e. Southampton Test	44,000	
Woolwich West	43,000	
Eastleigh	37,000	
etc.)		
5 CLPs would cast		125,000 votes
(assuming average membership of 2,500)		
74 CLPs would cast		1,110,000 votes
(assuming an average membership of 1,500)		
538 CLPs would cast		1,377,000 votes
(assuming the minimum affiliated membership of 256)		
623 CLPs would cast		**2,845,000 votes**

Compared with the present trade union affiliated membership, this scheme would give the CLPs approximately one-third of the total Conference vote rather than one-tenth. And this figure would move progressively towards one-half if the CLPs recruited more members; for example, if the 538 CLPs with low membership figures achieved a real membership of 1,000 each, then the CLP vote at Conference would be 8 million. It was felt, however, that the current affiliation fees that CLPs have to pay to the Party (£1.25p per member in 1980, and £2.50 per member in 1981) might well discourage parties from affiliating additional members above the minimum because of the heavy financial cost. Therefore we propose a sliding scale of affiliation fees for CLPs which we hope would deal with this problem, as follows:

£2.50 for each of the first 400 members = £1,000
£1.25 for each next 600 members = £720
£0.50 for each additional member over 1,000
(based on 1981 individual subscription of £5 p.a.)

The overall merits of this scheme are that it would substantially increase CLP voting strength in line with actual membership; it would be simple to introduce; and it would operate under the Party's present tules, without the need for cumbersome procedures.

Improvements to Conference Procedure

It is commonplace to blame the lack of correspondence between the decisions of Labour Party Conference and the actions of Labour Governments entirely on the attitudes of the Parliamentary leadership. In fact the situation is more complex, and at least two other factors play their part in undermining the legitimacy of Conference decisions.

First, Conference procedures are capricious: what emerges as a Conference policy may owe at least as much to the quirks of the compositing and voting processes as to the outcome of a political debate.

Secondly, by a process of feedback the Parliamentary leadership's dismissive attitude to Conference has encouraged Conference to regard itself more as a protest rally than a serious policy-making body, and this process has been aided and abetted by the NEC, who have too often encouraged Conference to vote on the spirit rather than the detail of resolutions. Consequently a vicious circle has developed in which Governments ignore Conference, while Conference too often produces policies which Governments feel inclined to ignore.

The decision of the 1979 Conference to give to the NEC ultimate responsibility for the contents of the Manifesto can be seen, however, as an attempt to make Conference behave more responsibly by giving it (through the NEC) greater responsibility. But it will only succeed in this as part of a larger package of

34

procedural reform. This section sets out a few ideas for such reform.

i. *Improving Policy Making*

1. *Opening all policy votes at Conference to public scrutiny*

The present system of "secret" voting was adopted in the early 1950s. The Group felt that the names of affiliated bodies should be put on voting cards, which would be open to public scrutiny. By making voting open, the accountability of both CLPs and trade unions to their members would be improved. At the moment, it is difficult to find out how each organisation has voted. The traditional argument over secret ballots is irrelevant, since the secret ballot aims to protect the individual voter and not the mandated delegate. (At the TUC, union delegations vote openly, by holding up their voting cards.)

2. *Availability of information*

All information that is available to the press (e.g. NEC decisions on Conference resolutions) should be given to delegates and not withheld as at present.

3. *Availability of subjects for debate*

The rules for compositing must be kept as relaxed as possible, to allow, for example, amendments to be used even if a main resolution fails because of the absence of its mover.

4. *Emergency Resolutions*

We would suggest that the rules relating to emergency resolutions be clarified, and that delegates are made aware of them at the beginning of Conference. The existing ambiguity about what qualifies as an emergency and who has the right to submit emergency resolutions should be cleared up.

5. *Remittance of Resolutions*

At present, the decision as to whether to remit a resolution or not rests with the mover, and if the mover refuses an NEC recommendation to remit, then Conference is usually advised to vote against the resolution. We felt the Conference itself should be allowed to vote on whether or not a resolution should be remitted.

6. Majority voting

The rule which lays down that only decisions carried by a two-thirds majority on a card vote can form part of the Party's Programme should be replaced by a rule which requires that the chairman declares when a two-thirds majority has been cast (this declaration being subject to a call for a card vote as at present). Currently, on policy matters, the card vote tends to be used only to decide sharply contested issues and where there is overwhelming support for a resolution no card vote will be called, so paradoxically it will not become part of the *Programme*.

7. Documents for consideration

NEC documents and statements which are to be brought before Conference should be issued far enough in advance for affiliated organisations to have the opportunity to move amendments. For a major document like *Labour's Programme* new procedures would be needed to reduce what could be a very larger number of amendments to a manageable set of choices. One possibility would be for Conference, a year before it was to adopt a new *Programme*, to elect a special committee which would have the responsibility of sifting the amendments and proposing draft composites for agreement by the relevant affiliated organisations.

ii. Conference, the PLP and the NEC

1. Conference Resolutions and the PLP

At present no means exist whereby Conference decisions can be formally conveyed to the PLP for consideration. When Labour is in office, resolutions critical of the Government go to ministers, but there is no communication with the PLP itself. Even when resolutions are sent direct to the PLP, these go to the Liaison Committee or to the Shadow Cabinet. They do not come to the PLP meeting and therefore do not have to be discussed.

The Group thought it was important to ensure that Conference resolutions were fed into PLP discussions so that the PLP would be made fully aware of the Party's views on particular matters.

2. Accountability and NEC and PLP Reports

One of the less satisfactory features of intra-party democracy in the past two decades has been the way in which the Reports

36

procedure has been undermined; it is no longer an effective instrument of accountability to Conference. It would be difficult (given the scope of the business) to get it back to the position of the early 1950s (when both PLP and NEC Reports were discussed as the first item of business on Monday morning), but some attempt must be made to put these reports under Conference scrutiny. The Group felt that sufficient time should be set aside at Conference to debate the NEC and PLP reports, with a clear right to refer back in whole or in part. It might be necessary to adopt a rule stating that if delegates wished individual paragraphs to be debated they would have to get the support of a minimum number of Conference delegates.

iii. Making Conference Procedures More Democratic

1. Opening Decisions of the Conference Arrangements Committee for Scrutiny

At present, the CAC has wide powers to exclude resolutions, without the Party being able to see the expressions of opinion contained in them. The Group felt that some procedure to decide which resolutions should be debated at Conference was essential as it was not acceptable that the CAC should be left to both devise and apply a classification system, since the "subjects" with the largest number of resolutions take priority in reaching the agenda.

We therefore recommend:

a. that a classification scheme, based on the sections into which Labour's programme is divided, should be submitted to all affiliated organisations who should themselves decide in which class their resolutions fell.

b. that the rules and guidelines used by the CAC should be submitted to Conference for approval.

c. The CAC should make available its rules regarding eligibility of resolutions and procedures of compositing, and publish all resolutions which it rules out of order with reasons given. In addition the first session at Conference (every day) should be devoted to the consideration of the CAC's detailed recommendations about the agenda. Conference would be asked to vote if necessary, after proper debate, on which subjects are to be debated and what resolutions disallowed.

2. Changing the Composition of the Conference Arrangements Committee

At present all five seats on the CAC are occupied by representatives of the trade unions, and it was agreed that the CLPs ought to have some representation on it. We therefore propose that in addition to 5 representatives from the trade unions (to be elected by the unions) there should be 5 CLP representatives (elected by the CLP delegates).

3. Standing Orders Committee Reports

These should be duplicated and issues to delegates each day (as is the practice in trade unions).

4. Publication of agenda

a. The publication dates of the first and second agendas should be brought forward to allow organisations more time for discussion.
b. All constitutional amendments, including those from the NEC, should be published in the first agenda and amendments to them permitted. The 1968 Conference ruling should be put on a more formal footing so that organisations are guaranteed the right to have their constitutional amendments debated and voted on (after the year's delay) if they so wish.
c. Resolutions ruled out of order should be published and Conference given a chance to vote on this in order to make the CAC more accountable.
d. There should be an automatic right for an issue to be debated if it attracts, say, 15 resolutions, amendments or constitutional amendments.

5. Discussion of Agenda by Conference

It was felt that the agenda and timetable for the week, stating which resolutions would be taken, should be submitted to Conference at a special first session. Both the NEC and affiliated organisations should be allowed to object to the draft agenda, but a minimum number of CLPs would have to support an objection before it was taken. Such a reform would both allow for the ventilation of grievances and, by its very existence, act as a restraint on the CAC's overall control of the agenda. It would also be helpful if the draft agenda indicating which subjects were likely to be discussed could be sent out to delegates two or three weeks in advance of Conference.

6. *Compositing*

a. Head Office should facilitate the exchange of draft composites in advance of the pre-Conference compositing meeting by supplying the addresses of the organisations involved. The possibility of compositing on major issues well in advance of conference should be seriously considered.

b. In situations where there is a clear difference of opinion within the compositing meeting, but not sufficient grounds for allowing two composites/resolutions, amendments to composites should be permitted. In addition, consideration should be given to the proposal that the NEC should have a limited right — under certain circumstances — within the same time limit as any other movers — to move amendments to composites/resolutions.

c. Provision should be made so that Conference is enabled to vote on a resolution/composite in parts. This procedure might be initiated at the request of the floor; by the NEC with the agreement of Conference; or in either of these ways.

7. *Amendments to Composite Motions*

This possibility was discussed by the Group, and we would suggest that the right to submit amendments to composite resolutions be confined to minority groups on compositing committees and to the NEC. This is an area that needs further study.

8. *Casting of votes*

There should be a procedure for immediate reference to the CAC of any alleged miscasting of votes, provided the complaint comes from a majority of the delegates directly concerned, and that the rules of their organisation specify that the casting of that vote was to be decided by its Conference delegation.

9. *Procedural Changes*

a. Conference Scheduling

The Group thought that the speeches of welcome could be drastically curtailed (if not scrapped altogether) and that evening sessions of Conference might be considered in order to accommodate all the business. In addition, NEC speeches should be kept within agreed time limits.

b. Movers of resolutions and constitutional amendments should have the right of reply — limited to 2 minutes.

10. Election of the NEC

Those who stand for the constituency section of the NEC should not necessarily be conference delegates.

Party Membership

Affiliated Membership

At present this is limited to organisations affiliated to the Labour Party at national level. However, in view of that fact that the rules* state that "Organisations affiliated to CLPs shall consist of any other organisation or branch thereof which the NEC deems eligible for affiliation" this need not necessarily be the case. Accordingly, it is at the NEC's discretion whether affiliation could be extended to groups broadly sympathetic to the Labour Party.

If this was done, then membership could encompass local pressure groups. This would offer new opportunities to make Labour Party membership more representative of under-privileged groups by inviting affiliation from ethnic minorities, women's groups, etc.

At the moment in accordance with Clause IV Section 1 of the Rules for CLPs, each of these pressure groups would be required:

a. to accept the programme, principles and policy of the Labour Party,
b. to agree to conform to the constitution and Standing Orders of the Labour Party and the Rules of this party.

It is proposed that paragraphs (a) and (b) should be relaxed so that any group broadly sympathetic (in the opinion of the NEC) to the aims and programmes of the Labour Party would be permitted to affiliate to CLPs. Once affiliated these organisations would be able to elect delegates to GCs in the same way as socialist societies (in accordance with the Labour Party Rules of up to a maximum of 5 delegates).

It is also proposed that workplace branches be treated in

*Clause III, Section 2, paragraph (f).

exactly the same manner, with an affiliation fee to be determined by the NEC. Workplace branches should therefore be open to all those interested in the Labour Party — irrespective of whether or not the union is affiliated nationally. Delegates and officers of the work place branches, however, would have to be individual Labour Party members.

Subscriptions

The existing subscriptions quite rightly allow for much lower rates for senior citizens. There is no logical reason why the same principle should not be extended to other under-privileged groups such as the unemployed, the recipients of supplementary benefits, the un-waged and low-waged.

Local Government Democracy

The gap between Parliamentary representatives and the National Party which often emerges after an Election is paralleled in many cases by the gap between a Council Labour Group and its own constituency parties and Local Government Committee or District Labour Party.

An experiment in local democracy pioneered by Lewisham Local Government Committee, at the instigation of West Lewisham CLP, contains the pattern of a desirable reform.

Essentially the Lewisham Local Government Committee held a one day policy-making Annual Delegate Conference for the Borough, run broadly along the lines of National Conference. It is intended to repeat this event annually. Each branch of each CLP was entitled to send 10 voting delegates, though party members were all entitled to attend as observers.

The advantages of transferring the major policy making function from a delegate Committee to an annual delegate Conference are very straightforward. A genuine rank and file involvement in policy making becomes possible, and the policy decisions themselves acquire a much greater legitimacy, are more widely understood in the Party and the community and are likely to be more effectively binding on local councillors. Trade union branches which are often disinclined to send active delegates to GCs might well be drawn into active participation in this annual forum because of its direct relationship with the work of the local Council.

For such a practice to be followed certain rule changes would be desirable. It would be sensible, for example, for an annual conference of this kind to elect its own Executive, to replace the Local Government Committee. Proper provision would have to be made for trade union representation — often very weak at Borough or District level.

In line with the Group's proposals for reforming the PLP the following recommendations are made with regard to the relationship between the Labour Group and the Borough Conference:

a. There should be full consultation between the Labour Group and the EC of the Borough Conference at regular intervals and there should always be full consultation between the Labour Group and the EC on all major decisions to be taken by the Labour Group.

b. The Borough Conference would receive a report from the Labour Group and this report would be debated and voted on section by section. At the same time, the EC of the Borough Conference would draw up a report of the year's activities of the Labour Group to be submitted to the Borough Conference.

c. Either the Borough Conference or an electoral college (a combination of the Borough Conference and the Labour Group) should elect the Leader of the Labour Group.

d. The standing orders of the Labour Group, which should be laid before the Borough Conference for approval (subject to overall approval by the NEC) should contain explicit recognition that it is the first duty of the Labour Group to implement local Party policy as set out in the Manifesto and supplemented by the decisions of the Borough Conference. The acceptance form for local government candidates should contain a specific commitment by the candidate to seek to implement the local policies of the Party as set out in the Manifesto and supplemented by the decisions of the Borough Conference.

e. Votes on key issues in the Labour Group should be recorded, and the lists of those voting for and against should be circulated with the full minutes of the Labour Group meetings which should be available to all Party members. (The provision for observers at Group meetings would continue.)

f. In order to prevent total domination of the Borough Conference by Councillors the Group felt that it should be stipulated that a certain proportion of the Borough Conference delegates (say 50%) should be lay representatives. All Councillors would in any case be ex-officio members of the Conference.

The Group recognised that the local government structure throughout the country was not exactly the same as in London;

there are several variations in the different regions. Nevertheless, in terms of the general spirit of the Group's recommendations it is possible to draw up analogous proposals to suit every variation. For instance, where a District Council straddles several CLPs there would be an annual District Conference, or where the boundaries of the District Council only cover one CLP that CLP would hold a District Conference which would have, say, 50 delegates, elected by the branches and affiliated organisations within that CLP.

The Group were only too aware that these proposals are only tentative. Nevertheless, they were strongly of the opinion that the Enquiry should examine the principle, and investigate the changes in Rule necessary to bring about this extension of democracy and accountability within the relationship between the Party and its representatives in local government.

BACKGROUND PAPERS

I Parliamentary Candidates

The Group considered many aspects of this matter. Much of the discussion centred on the question of which body should have the final responsibility for selection and reselection, and one member of the Group recorded disagreement with the majority decision. Nevertheless, it was generally felt that the arguments in favour of selection remaining the prerogative of the General Committee strongly outweighed those advocating some form of 'primary' system. The arguments on both sides are set out in detail below.

Those who argued in favour of selection remaining the final responsibility of the GC did not do so uncritically. There are many improvements that can and should be made in the various procedures associated with the selection process. These are also set out in detail below.

But first we will focus on the more fundamental question.

Who should select the Parliamentary candidate?

Basically this question has come to revolve around whether the General Committee (GC) should, or should not, continue to be the body finally responsible for the selection and reselection of Parliamentary candidates. We will attempt to summarise the arguments for and against the present system, in this way to show that the former outweight the latter.

In practice the arguments against the GC continuing to have final responsibility cannot be separated from arguments in favour of this responsibility being transferred to the membership at large, and for our purposes these arguments will be taken together. These arguments have been many and varied, but can be summarised as follows:

From the supporters of the Campaign for Labour Victory

i. GCs are small and unrepresentative.

ii. GCs are open to influence and takeover by small groups.

iii. Few GCs go through a genuine selection process.

iv. Membership of GCs is not a test of party activity; some hard working members are excluded.

v. The MP must have "independence", since he/she acquires knowledge "which is far beyond what the average activist can hope to obtain" (letter in *The Guardian* 5/12/79).

vi. The GC system is described by many supporters of CLV as "elitist".

Some of the above arguments can be found in an article by John Cartwright (*Labour Weekly*, 2/11/79), others appear in CLV literature or in their press mouthpieces — especially the editorial columns of *The Guardian* and Ronald Butt (*The Sunday Times*, 23/12/79).

In his article, Butt even called on the Tories to add their weight to the fight to save Labour's "moderates" — "It becomes a question for all responsible politicians how they can preserve a moderate Labour Party. How, in other words, could primaries (of Labour Party members) be achieved? . . . Mrs Thatcher and the Tories should think about this because a moderate Labour Party is in their own interest as well as the nation's."

From some supporters of the Labour Co-ordinating Committee and the ILP Group ("Labour Leader")

(Who advocate allowing every member to attend the final selection meeting with safeguards to prevent 'packing', for instance attendance at 3 ward meetings.)

i. The GC system is based on an elitist notion; it suggests that members of GCs have "superior capacities" to those of the ordinary members, whereas "the proud principle of the Labour Party has always been that all members enjoy equal rights".

ii. Members of GCs cannot be mandated in the choice of MP and are therefore making personal choices.

iii. The vote at the GC is secret.

iv. Many of the candidates at the final selection meeting have not been interviewed by branches.

v. Reselection means an increase in membership and these new members should not be denied involvement in the selection process, which in turn will further increase membership.

vi. To talk of influence by the media is a dangerous argument. It can be levelled with equal force against the universal franchise, the extension of voting for the Party leader outside the House of Commons and mass meetings in factories.

These arguments can most readily be found in an article by Frances Morrell and Brian Sedgemore (*The Guardian,* 26/11/79).

The arguments in favour of the GC continuing to be the body finally responsible for the selection and reselection of Parliamentary candidates can be summarised as follows:

i. *Accountability*

The struggle for reselection gained such massive support because it was seen as a means through which the Party might achieve the implementation of Party policies, after a continuing series of object lessons since 1964 which revealed the total impotence of the Party in this direction. Only the knowledge that our policies will be implemented will recreate a mass crusading party. A repeat of the '64-79 pattern would be disastrous. And yet this is precisely what a retreat from selection by the GC would mean.

The GC — by its elected composition, its frequent meetings and its close contact with the MP — is the only body able to properly monitor the MP's actions between elections and, therefore, the members of the GC are in the best position to have the responsibility of reselection. But much more than this there would be no accountability if the monitoring body ceased to be the selecting body. If the GC ceased to be the latter the MP would be at liberty to completely ignore the GC and merely make an appeal to a mass meeting once every 4/5 years, at which many would be voting on a 'first impression' basis. There would be no accountability whatsoever and since the GC's role is to ensure the adherence of the MP to Party policy there would — *inevitably* given the pressures in the opposing direction — be little or no implementation of those Labour Party policies that seriously threatened the Establishment.

Accountability is only meaningful if it exists as a continuous monitoring process with effective sanctions. The supporters of 'primaries' must surely admit that it would be impossible in practice to have a regular series of mass meetings which would effectively monitor the MP. Such meetings would eventually become small and unrepresentative, with a consequent loss of continuity, and they would be ignored with impunity by the MP. Neither would it be practical (or effective) to substitute ward and branch meetings for these regular mass meetings, such that the MP reported to every ward and branch meeting in order that the latter might also become monitoring bodies. It seems hardly necessary to point out that the argument we are making revolves around the function that the GC and its members play and does not infer that the latter are in any way 'superior' to other party members. The charge of elitism is completely beside the point.

The supporters of the Campaign for Labour Victory are well aware of the significance of the accountability argument. In *The Guardian* of 9 July 1979, Shirley Williams had the following to say — "Mandatory reselection would, of course, make MPs more accountable to their GCs". But she went much further than this and added "it would turn MPs into little more than delegates from their GCs".

ii. *General Committees are responsible for all decisions*

Almost since its inception, the Party has had a well-defined system of delegate democracy. The process is quite clear and straightfoward: the members of the branches and affiliates of the Party take decisions together at the level of the branch and these decisions are then conveyed, via their own delegates to the General Committee, to the Constituency Party. If the branch so chooses, moreover, its delegates will be mandated to speak and vote in favour of the branch decision. It is thus the General Committee which has the responsibility for reconciling the various viewpoints of the branches and affiliates — and for reaching decisions in the light of these viewpoints. And this applies to *all* decisions — whether on constitutional matters, resolutions to Conference, or on the management of the Constituency Party itself.

There seems to be no justification for seeking to abstract just this one decision — the selection of a Parliamentary candidate — from these well-understood and well-organised procedures. Indeed, to do so would not only weaken the authority of the General Committees; it would also tend to undermine the authority or democratic credentials of our system of delegate democracy itself. Delegate democracy, it would appear, is simply not good enough, not democratic enough, for it to be used for major decisions at Constituency level, despite the fact that the Party's own Annual Conference — the sovereign body of the Party — is based on precisely the same procedure.

iii. *The GC represents all sections of the Party*

All sections of the Party and affiliated organisations are represented on the GC which reflects the Labour Party's federated structure. As a result each has a meaningful voice in all the affairs of the Constituency. 'Primaries' destroy this important principle and are particularly discriminatory against the Trade Unions. Trade Unions are represented at Constituency level by delegates chosen in numbers which reflect the number of trade unionists who, while not necessarily individual members of the Party, pay the political levy and live in the Constituency or are registered as electors there. If the selection of candidates were confined only to individual members then the trade union wing of the Party would, to a large degree, be disenfranchised.

A second point arises from the GC's federated structure; this is that the GC brings together the continuing collective discussion of political issues by the ward branches, trade union branches, co-op parties, etc. It is, therefore, the natural point of contact between the CLP and its MP.

iv. *The problem of 'packing'*

'Primaries' would mean that selection meetings would tend to become tests of organisation; those best at getting members to attend would win and in this competition those Parliamentary candidates who were well heeled might be more equal than others. Since the Trade Unions would be denied the share of the vote that selection by the GC ensures them, there is no doubt that they would be tempted to organise the flooding of the selection conference in order to obtain/retain a sponsored MP. There have been several examples of this even with the present system, and although the recent rule changes have made this more difficult further safeguards are required.

v. *Wide opportunities to interfere with normal Labour Party Procedures*

The bitter experience of Newham North East should not be ignored. It only takes one complaint to land the Party in the courts. As the Secretary of Newham North East has pointed out (*Tribune* 30/11/79) one complainant is more likely to be found in a CLP of several hundred members than on a GC of some 60 members. Not only is this obvious statistically but also because of the greater restraint due to psychological and political pressures acting on a delegate to a GC. With a 'primary' system a CLP will have to be so well organised that its secretary knows exactly and precisely the names and addresses of every party member who has paid the minimum subscription for the year (without the possibility of any slip-up whatsoever) and the party will have to be rich enough to send out the convening notices by recorded delivery (the only cast-iron way of being safe).

The attempted safeguard against 'packing' at the 'primary', namely that at least 3 ward meetings must have been attended, immeasurably increases the likelihood of court action. It would be very difficult to keep a completely accurate check of attendance at every ward and branch meeting; and there would be a built-in potential for aggravation at every one of these meetings. The complaints and the possibility of court action would give the press a field day.

The 'primaries' themselves would also be wide open to influence by the press. This is a real danger, as anyone who watched the Bob Wright-Terry Duffy battle will vouch. The GC delegates are, of course, also open to influence by the press but the GC system, which has been hammered out by the Party during its long struggle, does, for that very reason, to some extent counteract the anti-socialist environment in which we exist. This is precisely why it is so vilified by the Tory press.

Assessed in the abstract 'primaries' may appear to be very democratic, but democratic institutions cannot be assessed in this way. They must be assessed in the social and historical situation in which they exist, or will exist. If this is done in the case of 'primaries' the reality diverges from the appearance.

Selection Procedures

The Group discussed many proposals for improving the various procedures associated with the selection process. The following is a summary of those on which there was general agreement.

   i. GCs should examine ways of increasing their membership so as to allow the maximum possible participation by active members.

   ii. All closing dates for nominations should be published in *Labour Weekly.*

   iii. Each potential nominee should be given a list of affiliated organisations and secretaries' addresses and telephone numbers.

   iv. Nominees should be required to produce written political statements, to be circulated to all branches prior to selection meetings.

   v. All nominees should submit sufficient curricular vitae to the CLP Secretary, giving full details of all offices held and for how long.

   vi. A CLP involved in selecting a Parliamentary candidate should be entitled to contact prospective nominees' own CLPs for the purposes of obtaining factual information only, about those nominees' length of membership, offices held, etc., with the proviso that the nominees should be allowed to see the replies from their own CLPs and be able to comment on them before they are sent to the selecting CLP.

   vii. Each affiliated organisation/branch making a nomination must have a selection conference.

   viii. Both the branch selection meeting and the GC final selection meeting should try to combine individual interviews with panel discussions between nominees.

   ix. Branches should be permitted to discuss the merits of the nominees before deciding whom to nominate, but this principle should not be extended to the final selection meeting.

   x. The Executive Committee of the GC must invite all the nominees for interview before shortlisting.

   xi. Shortlisting by the Executive Committee should be by a single ballot, i.e., single, first-past-the-post ballot, rather than by an exhaustive eliminating ballot, to reduce the opportunities for tactical voting. It should also be laid down that the members of the Executive Committee should not be compelled to use their full number of votes: at present it is not uncommon for them to be instructed to vote against their wishes so as to use up all their votes, despite this 'ruling' being quite unfounded.

xii. Branches and affiliated organisations should be allowed to call together short-listed nominees to interview them (Branches could meet jointly if necessary). It was the view of some members of the Group that branches and affiliated organisations should be able to mandate their delegates to the final selection conference following such a meeting.

xiii. A CLP must always hold a bona fide selection conference with a representative shortlist of nominees, unless only one nominee offers himself or herself for nomination.

xiv. A copy of the NEC guidelines relating to the final selection meeting, which are currently available to Regional Organisers, should be given to members at the beginning of the selection procedure, and should be published in the NEC Report each year.

xv. The Group recognised that mandatory reselection immeasurably increased the potential for the abuses 'flooding'/'packing' the GC for the final selection meeting. This problem has already been recognised and the 1978 Annual Conference carried a constitutional amendment, which laid down that to be entitled to attend and vote at the final selection meeting, a member of the GC must have been a member of that CLP for at least 12 months prior to the date of the final selection meeting, and have attended at least one previous meeting of the GC. The Group felt that the latter safeguard was not sufficient, especially given that whereas the 1978 rules had 2 mandatory meetings associated with the reselection process, this was reduced to one meeting at the 1979 Annual Conference. The Group propose that the rules should be altered so as to insist that a member of the GC should have had to attend at least 3 meetings of the GC in the previous 12 months prior to the final selection meeting. The position of new delegates, who might not be able to fulfil this requirement – for instance, if the selection process was initiated shortly after the Party's AGM — was discussed, but it was felt that for the rule to operate it would have to be strictly applied. In general, CLPs would not initiate the selection process shortly after the AGM.

xvi. As a further safeguard against 'flooding'/'packing' it was felt that the rules regarding affiliation to CLPs should be tightened up. Where an organisation is already affiliated and increases its affiliation, its vote (i.e., number of delegates) at the GC should remain based on its former affiliation for a period of one year — in line with CLP affiliations to the National Party and their vote at Conference. New affiliates to a CLP should be immediately entitled to play a full role in the GC, except in the event of a Parliamentary selection procedure, in which case they should be disbarred for one year.

xvii. The Group also recognised that abuses occur in respect of the payment of delegates' expenses. It was noted that in some CLPs it is traditional to pay delegates who have travel difficulties or loss of earnings problems, as a result of working on night shift, etc. It was agreed that in these circumstances CLPs should pay expenses. However, this was not the same as cases in which affiliated organisations pay the expenses of all their delegates. It was felt that this was not acceptable and that a rule preventing this should be formulated if it was practicable to do so.

xviii. As a condition of nomination as a Parliamentary candidate, an individual should provide an official signed declaration that he or she, if elected, will abide by, and seek to implement, the policies of the Party as set out in the Manifesto and the Labour Programme, supplemented by resolutions of Annual Conference.

Positive Discrimination

The majority of the Group felt that a further small, but very significant, change should be made to the selection procedure, namely, that constitutional amendments should be brought before Conference which will lay down that all shortlists for Parliamentary selections should include at least one member of the two disadvantaged majority sections of the population — manual workers and women — unless no such applications are forthcoming. (In the absence of any branch or affiliated organisation making such nominations the EC of the General Committee should be empowered to make such nominations from among those who have put their names forward.)

It was felt very strongly by some members of the Group that the implications of such a change would reach far beyond the limited confines of the Parliamentary selection procedure. It would show a commitment on behalf of the Labour Party that it was prepared to actively take up and campaign on issues affecting these majority sections. The Labour vote amongst the working class and women will only be significantly increased by policies in their direct interest.

For too long the widely recognised need for the positions of power and prestige in the Labour Party to be more representative has been left to mere exhortation to CLPs and trade unions to put forward more manual workers and women. But it is painfully obvious that mere exhortation is nowhere near enough. Some 65 per cent of the population are manual workers and their families, and they deliver something approaching 90 per cent of the Labour votes. Yet out of a total of 268 Labour MPs only about 50 were manual workers prior to becoming an MP, and only 11 Labour MPs are women (*Labour Research* July 1979). The consequences of this dominance of the PLP by middle class men can readily be appreciated, and it helps to explain the lack of commitment by Labour Governments to radical social change. Built-in institutional procedures are necessary that will begin to counteract the discrimination and, at the same time, give manual workers and women much needed encouragement. These proposals are only a small step, but they will stimulate Labour Party members to question themselves and their prejudices and, in addition, they will give manual workers and women slightly better chances of being selected. Many members of the Labour Party are unaware of the profound depth of the discrimination suffered by these majority sections. And even amongst those who are aware of this, there is a widely held myth that the discrimination somehow stops at the door of the Labour Party. It may be true that the Labour Party can boast of formal equality, but this has also been the proud boast of other parts of society, for instance, particularly of the education system. But if we look for example at university entrants, for which accurate statistics are kept, the hollowness of the claim is soon exposed.

The proportion of university students from a manual working class background is a little less than 25 per cent. This proportion has hardly changed since the early 1930s, despite the massive increase in higher education places in recent years. Indeed, according to a study of admissions to Scottish universities in 1962 and 1972, made at Glasgow University, there was a 17.1 per cent decline in working class students between those years. In fact it was noted that there were less students from working class backgrounds at Scottish universities now than during the latter half of the 19th century.

Brian Simon once made a calculation which precisely pinpointed the staggering discrimination within society. He showed that within the state education system a middle class boy in Carmarthenshire had a colossal 180 times greater chance of gaining university admission than a girl from the East End of London. This is a measure of the discrimination that a policy of positive discrimination would be bringing attention to.

In the Labour Party, as in education, formal equality does not counteract the discrimination. What is required is a positive intervention that will move us towards *real* equality.

II The National Executive Committee

Role, Authority and Composition

This section is in two parts. The first deals with the role and authority of the NEC; the second deals with its composition. The theme underlying both sections, however, is the same: the need to strengthen the authority of the NEC, vis-a-vis the Parliamentary Labour Party — and in particular vis-a-vis the Parliamentary Leadership. Only if we do so, it is suggested, can the NEC play its part, *effectively,* in ensuring that Labour Governments actually implement Party policy as well as talk about it.

We do not, in this section, consider the general *administrative* role of the NEC, either financial or organisational. For as important as these issues are, the problems associated with them are not necessarily linked directly either to the authority of the NEC or to its composition. Indeed, that the NEC is, and should be, the administration authority of the Party has not been seriously challenged, even by the PLP. Our concern here is with policy. What changes should we make to give the NEC the authority and status it needs to deal with a Labour Government as an equal?

1. The Role of the NEC

The basic role of the NEC was concisely set out in the Report of the Committee of Enquiry, in 1968:

"In the Party Constitution the National Executive Committee is described as the 'administrative authority' of the Party; but the words used in detailing the powers and duties of the National Executive make it obvious that 'administrative' is used in the widest possible sense. The powers of the National Executive include the right to propose to the Annual Conference 'such amendments to the Constitution, Rules and Standing Orders as may be deemed desirable' and 'such resolutions and declarations affecting the Programme, Principles and Policy of the Party . . . as may be necessitated by political circumstances'. *In practice the National Executive provides the positive leadership of the Party.*"

Since the publication of that Report, a number of changes have been made to strength the 'positive leadership' role of the NEC in terms of policy development within the Party:

First, the terms of reference for the post of General Secretary were considerably widened, in 1972, to include a direct reference to "responsibility for propagating and seeking the implementation of the policies of the Party", (The General Secretary does, incidentally, attend all Shadow Cabinet meetings, with a clear right to put forward the views of the Party.);

Second, a new emphasis has been given to Clause V of the Party Constitution, which lays down that there should be a Party Programme, on the basis of which the Manifesto should be prepared: and the NEC has thus given a much higher priority than hitherto to the formulation of policy and to the presentation to Conference of major statements outlining detailed Party commitments;

Third, the NEC has supported this development by an·extensive network of policy sub-committees and study groups, involving upwards of 500 experts of one kind or another drawn from the Party — including Ministers, MPs, councillors, academics, trade unionists and representatives from a wide range of pressure groups;

Fourth, the NEC – and to a lesser extent, the General Secretary – have sought to impress upon the Parliamentary Leadership the need to adhere to Party policy – and they have done so both publicly and forcefully;

Fifth, an attempt has been to associate the TUC as closely as possible with the various policies which were emerging as a result of the NEC studies – through, for example, the TUC-Labour Party Liaison Committee, through joint NEC/TUC studies (e.g. on shipbuilding) and by including TUC representation on all NEC sub-committees and groups. (Unfortunately, this approach only really succeeded whilst we were in opposition.)

Despite these developments, however, the 'leadership role' of the NEC on policy matters has not – in terms of practical results – amounted to very much. Why has this been so? In a note to the NEC by the Party's Research Secretary (reprinted in the IWC book *What Went Wrong*), six major areas of concern were listed:

(i) *"The status of the NEC and Party vis-a-vis the Cabinet:* . . . The status of the NEC was, in practice, that of a mere pressure group, just one among many . . . The outcome of the numerous NEC delegations, meetings, etc., was little different from that of other pressure groups: a few minor successes perhaps, but little in the way of changing the *direction* of Government policy."

(ii) *"The lack of involvement of the Cabinet in Party policy-making:* . . . Although Ministers were heavily represented on our sub-committees and study groups, this did not mean that the Government became committed in any way to the policies which emerged. There was certainly no real sense of *joint* decision-making: the Government displayed little serious interest in the policy-making effort of the NEC and the Party (Labour's Programme, for example, was never considered or discussed by the Cabinet)."

(iii) *"The lack of involvement by the Party in Government decision-making:* . . . There was little effective *advance* consultation by the Government with the NEC, especially about major policy developments; and certainly seldom – if ever – on a basis of trying to reach agreed, joint decisions on what should be done. In many cases, indeed, the NEC was at a disadvantage compared to other major interest groups, including the CBI, the City, the TUC and others."

(iv) *"The procedure for drawing up the Manifesto:* . . . On the same day that the Manifesto was to be launched (at a Press Conference in the evening) NEC members – apart from the handful on the Drafting Committee – had their *first* opportunity to see the draft manifesto . . . Thus, despite all the planning of the previous two years, all the meetings, all the decisions, the NEC had been set up to agree the very kind of Manifesto, in the very circumstances, it had always hoped to avoid."

[Note: The problem here is *not* just one of procedure: for it was always unrealistic to expect the Government to make a complete U-turn, in favour of Party policy, just for the sake of drafting the Manifesto. And the same will be true for the Shadow Cabinet, next time around. For the Manifesto has to be seen as the end result of a long process of argument and discussion within the Party, with the Leadership and MPs not only accepting, *in advance,* the primary of Party policy, but also accepting that it is their duty to expound these policies, once agreed, at every opportunity.]

(v.) "*Lack of consultation with Party members in the development of NEC policy:* . . . In the *preparation* of its detailed statements, the NEC relies heavily on the relatively small number of researchers, back-benchers, etc., who serve on the advisory sub-committees. No procedures have been devised to provide for systematic consultation within the Party *before* statements are issued as policy. Neither have we been able to provide properly for political education within the Party about the new policies whilst they were still under discussion. As a result, we have failed to build up either the support or the understanding we need, within the Party, to help carry out policies through into the Manifesto and Government action."

(vi) "*The status of NEC statements and the procedure for endorsement:* . . . In the process of endorsing NEC policy, Conference has all too often been expected to adopt – without amendment and with minimal debate – lengtny documents, even though these documents might have been circulated far too late for proper discussion and decision by affiliated organisations, prior to Conference. In the case of the numerous NEC statements issued between Conferences, moreover, Conference is not consulted at all."

To these six, another problem could also be noted: the way in which *the close alliance between the Cabinet and TUC leaders was used to further undermine the status of the NEC – and to deflect Party criticism.* As a result, the effectiveness of the TUC-Labour Party Liaison Committee was sharply reduced; and the Government was also able to use the joint agreements reached within the Committee ("The Next Three Years" and "Into the Eighties" for example) as a means of watering down Party policy. This was so despite the fact that the Government did not accept that it was bound by these joint agreements, either in terms of Government action or even in agreeing proposals for the Manifesto.

It is obvious from the above – and indeed from the record – that the NEC has neither the authority nor the status to play the "positive leadership" role which is needed on issues of policy: it cannot effectively act as 'custodian of Conference decisions'. But it is also clear that it is not even equipped to generate the kind of widespread support and understanding in the Party which is needed to make its policies stick. On this latter point, the NEC has now agreed new procedures for consultation on policy, prior to the submission of statements to Conference; and we also set out in a separate section our proposals for improving the way in which the Party comes to its firm decisions on policy statements and resolutions.

The Authority of the NEC

On the question of authority, however, it is important to be clear just how far we consider it is possible – or even desirable – to enhance the powers of the NEC. There are, indeed, a number of alternatives. For example, the Party could:

- adopt the position of the Communist Party, and give the NEC a similar all-powerful role, subject to Conference, to that of the CP's Central Committee. With this model, all levels of the Party would be expected to take their cue from the centre; and once policy has been decided at the centre, public criticism and debate is expected to cease;
- provide the NEC with similar powers and authority on policy questions – including on the implementation of policy – as those enjoyed on issues of administration in the Party. This is close to the first option above, but stops short of complete control;
- to restore the position of the Executive to that which was assumed to exist in the thirties and forties (less a matter of constitutional provision than a certain 'understanding' about the role of the extra-Parliamentary wing);
- develop a new position, less dependent on the good sense and good behaviour of the Parliamentary Leadership, and much more on clear and explicit provisions in the Constitution and Standing Orders of the Party (including those of the PLP). This would establish the NEC as the prime authority as regards interpreting the decisions of Conference (i.e. on what the broad policy of the party *is*); and also establish the NEC as an equal partner as regards the *implementation* of policy, with the tactics and strategy of the PLP and its leaders (in Govern-

61

ment and in Opposition) becoming subject to joint regulation and joint control.

Given the traditions and principles of the Party, there is little real point in considering the first option at any length. Certainly few Labour Party members would accept the 'democratic centralism' which is implicit in this approach.[1]

Problems with a centralist approach

But would the second option fare much better? It would, after all, involve the NEC having the final say, and being able to give *instructions* on, the following:

- on how the PLP responds as an Opposition to Tory initiatives — both in terms of statements and votes (subject, of course, to the usual caveat on issues of conscience);
- on the activities and policies of a Labour Cabinet, as regards Ministerial Statements, legislation and the rest, with the Whips taking their cue directly from the NEC;
- on the activities and policies of Labour Groups, whether in control of their local authorities or not;
- on the activities and policies (subject to their right to submit resolutions) of all local parties, including whether or not they should support certain campaigns at local level, etc.

It is extremely unlikely that the Party would be prepared to go this far. For the problem with any centralist approach is that *there are, in practice, a number of different "centres of authority" in the Labour Movement, all with their own kind of 'legitimacy':*

First, there are the individual CLPs, who will always insist on their right to choose their candidates, mount their own campaigns, support causes dear to their own hearts, and to (jointly) determine the policies of their Labour Groups.

Second, there are the local authority Labour Groups themselves — which include councillors and council leaders not noted for their willingness to toe a line handed down to them from the centre, even from Party Conference. And this is despite the fact that councillors have for years had to face periodic reselection, and that they very often work closely with the local parties.

Third, there is the PLP, which will always seek, at the very least, a degree of genuine partnership as far as the implementation of policy is concerned: and this will be so *a fortiori* if it establishes its own domestic procedures. Indeed, it will be so even if the PLP comes to mirror much more closely opinion in the Party, whether of activists or of Party members in general.

Fourth, there is the Parliamentary Leadership, which, if it were to be elected by a combination of the PLP and conference (or an electoral college) would be even more likely to insist on its rights to be involved in deciding tactics and priorities within the broad strategy laid down by Conference. (As a Cabinet, it would be even more determined to defend its rights as a collective entity responsible to Parliament.)

And fifth, there are the trade unions. On the one hand there are those affiliated to the Party, a powerful group in their own right — as witness the TULV — bodies which are not likely to concede that their existing representation on the NEC diminishes in any way their right to share *directly* in the decision making of Governments, whether through the TUC or otherwise; on the other, there is the trade union movement as a whole — organised through the TUC — which has, after all, a growing proportion of its membership in unions not affiliated to the Party (and thus not even indirectly represented on the NEC).

Given the existence of these alternative 'centres of authority', it seems highly unlikely that the Party would accept the NEC having such wide-ranging powers. And this would be so, we suspect, even if it was only the PLP which was to be subject to this new authority.

The 'Attlee' model

An alternative approach might be simply to revert to the position accepted by the Party — including the Parliamentary Leadership — during the thirties and fourties. In essence, this accepted the supremacy of Conference, at least as far as the principles and basic policies of the Party were concerned: but the Parliamentarians themselves decided upon their timing and application. And the PLP remained an autonomous body regulating its own internal affairs.

In this context, Lewis Minkin, in his book *The Labour Party Conference*, reminds us of the 1933 NEC statement "Labour and Government" — and especially of provision number seven:

"The policy to be pursued by the Labour Government would be that laid down in Resolutions of the Annual Conference and embodied in the General Election Manifesto. The King's Speech would, from year to year, announce the instalments of the Party's policy with which the Government proposed to deal. Where questions arise for decision on which Party policy had not been declared they would be dealt with by discussion with the appropriate bodies."

Lewis Minkin also notes that Attlee, in 1937, set out very clearly the constitutional relationship assumed for the various bodies of the Party: ". . . the Labour Party Conference lays down the policy of the Party, and issues instructions which must be carried out by the Executive, the affiliated organisations, and its representatives in Parliament and on local authorities".

On the other hand, in line with traditional practice, Attlee made it plain that: "Action in the House is a matter for the Parliamentary Party, the members of which decide on the application of Party policy. The Labour Party Executive is the body to interpret policy between Conferences, *but in its own sphere the Parliamentary Party is supreme*" (our emphasis). Nevertheless, "the final authority of the Labour Party is the Party Conference". As Lewis Minkin comments: "As a statement of the Party's theory of government, it accurately represented the balance of authority and discretion, principle and specificity understood by the majority of leaders and Party members in the 1930s".

There are, however, two major problems with this approach. First, unless there are clear provisions in the Constitution to back up these "assumptions" about inter-Party relationships, we are completely dependent on the goodwill of the Parliamentary Leadership — and on *their* interpretation of what Conference has decided. Second, the NEC is effectively left out in the cold: it is given no clear role as the interpreter of Conference decisions (even as regards its own statements of policy) — which, given the vagueness of so much of the policy adopted by Conference, is of critical importance. Neither is it seen as an authoritative source of policy in between Conferences — for example in responding to major events and developments. As Attlee was later to emphasise, on the occasion of the controversy over remarks made by Harold Laski during the 1945 election campaign:

"Neither by decision of the annual party conference or by any provision in the party constitution is the Parliamentary Labour Party answerable to, or under the direction of the National Executive Committee. Within the programme adopted by the annual party conference *the*

Parliamentary Labour Party has complete discretion in its conduct of Parliamentary business and in the attitude it should adopt to legislation tabled by other parties. The standing orders which govern its activities are drawn up and determined by the Parliamentary Labour Party itself." (Our emphasis.)

Clearly, the Attlee model does represent a move in the right direction: and it is certainly superior to the practice of the PLP in the sixties and seventies. Nonetheless, it is suggested, it does not go anywhere near far enough in providing a clear policy role for the NEC.

New 'Sanctions' on the PLP?

One approach might be simply to beef up the Attlee approach by devising new "sanctions" which could be applied by the Party against the PLP – should the latter ignore Conference decisions. And a number of suggestions for such sanctions are under discussion within the Party and set out in other chapters. These include mandatory reselection; mandatory declarations by all Parliamentary candidates; putting the PLP Standing Orders to Conference for approval and amendment; regular reports to the Party on the record of the PLP; new procedures at Conference for scrutinising the work of the PLP; open voting at PLP meetings; and the reform of the PLP itself (including the election of the Cabinet).

All of these reforms, certainly, are necessary to help tip the balance of power away from the Parliamentary wing of the Party. They could also help enormously to strengthen the authority of the NEC vis-a-vis the Parliamentary Leadership. But would they be enough in themselves? For there would still be the need for an executive body of some kind, at national level, to conduct the day-to-day, month-to-month policy business of the Party – just as there is a need for a management committee (GC or GMC) at constituency level. And this includes the preparation of coherent policy statements to Conference, drafting the Manifesto and *effectively* scrutinising the day-to-day work of Labour Governments.

The view of the majority of the Group, therefore, is that further additional reforms are needed to strengthen the role of the extra-parliamentary party as an instrument of initiative and authority. The need is for an executive body – the NEC – which is, after all, elected from and responsible to the Party's own "Parliament".

JOINT CONTROL

One line of reform would be to borrow the concept of "joint control" from the Party's own policies on industrial democracy. As far as industrial democracy is concerned, this approach accepts that, as a fact of life, there are 'two sides' in industry — management and workers — and that each has a 'legitimate' interest: sometimes conflicting, sometimes not. And it suggests that the best way to do business under these circumstances — that is, with competing centres of authority and loyalty — is through a *continuing process of negotiation*. This would be undertaken with the clear understanding that, in the absence of joint agreement, no action should be taken by either side (unless, of course, there is a total breakdown in negotiations, when either side can withdraw and apply sanctions). The aim, in essence, is to establish a process of *joint regulation* over as many areas of decision-making as possible: and the method is to rely not on 'consultation' but on negotiation, with the aim of striking jointly agreed bargains and deals which can be honoured by both sides.

Translating this concept into Party democracy would mean our acceptance of the need for a similar process of continuous negotiation between the various centres of authority — and, in particular, between the two most important of them, the NEC, and the PLP.[2] Again, as with industrial democracy, the aim would be joint regulation — in this case over such major activities as policy development and policy implementation; and, in place of the usual vague commitment to 'consultation', we are here talking about genuine negotiations in order to arrive at agreements on what a Labour Government should actually do.

The implications for both the PLP Leadership and for the NEC, are very radical indeed:

Labour in Government

Joint control would involve a major change in the way that Parliamentary democracy works, or is meant to work, in this country. In effect, it would mean the end of the present system of Cabinet Government, at least whilst Labour is in power. The

Cabinet, for example, would cease to be responsible (even in theory) only to Parliament and become instead directly accountable also to the Party: and all of the conventions and secrecy which go to support Cabinet Government — and which make it impossible for the Party in practice to help shape the policy and practice of Labour Governments — would have to be abandoned. Similarly, individual Ministers would be expected to answer not only to Parliament, the Cabinet, and the PM, but also to the Party. *In short, the Cabinet, and all Labour Ministers, would be bound, by the Party Constitution, to govern the country in joint stewardship with the representatives of the Party.*

What would be the nature of the new conventions which would bind Labour governments? We list below some examples:[3]

— A statutory *policy liaison committee* (or somesuch), drawn equally from the NEC and Cabinet, shall meet before each Cabinet; it shall have before it the agenda and papers to be considered by the Cabinet (subject only to the limitations on secrecy — for example, on defence — accepted by Conference in the Party's current policy on information disclosure). Any agreements reached within this committee will be *ad referendum* to the Cabinet: but wherever Cabinet endorsement is not forthcoming, then no action will be taken pending further negotiations with the Party.[4]

— At the commencement of each session of Parliament, the PM shall informally *consult* with the NEC (or its officers, or the policy liaison committee) on proposals for inclusion in the Programme of Legislation (the Queen's Speech); following these consultations, the *draft Speech* will be laid before a joint meeting of the full NEC and Cabinet (or joint committees thereof) so that the actual text may be jointly agreed, line by line.

— Chairmen of Cabinet Committees will be expected to keep appropriate NEC members and Party officials informed on the progress of business — and to seek agreement with the NEC (or with the appropriate NEC committee) — without waiting for the issues to come before the full Cabinet. Disagreements will be referred to the policy liaison committee.

— No *Government statement,* no *Bill,* no *Budget,* no major *Government action* of any kind will be made or issued before joint agreement has been reached with the NEC or appropriate

NEC committee. (Certain safeguards will no doubt be needed on Budget details, such as excise duties, etc.).

— The above will apply equally to the seeking of any *Parliamentary alliances*; to the use of any kind of *referenda* (including the questions to be put before the electorate); to the granting of *honours* and distinctions; to the timing of the General Election; etc., etc.

— Wherever appropriate — and especially where this is disagreement or lack of enthusiasm on the part of the Party — the Government could be entitled to publish its proposals in 'consultative' form, as a Green Paper, Consultation Paper, or whatever; but the reservations of the Party should also be noted in such documents.

— Government Ministers would be expected to play a major role in assisting the NEC in its development of Party policy: and this would include their active participation on the advisory sub-committees and study groups of the NEC. Any serious disagreements should be referred upwards to the policy liaison committee — and especially wherever the issue concerns the preparation of draft NEC *statements*. (A more relaxed approach can apply to NEC Discussion Documents: but even here, the Documents should include, openly, the reservations put forward by Ministers.)

The context of these new conventions would, of course, be the overriding requirement that policy is determined by Conference. The policies to which the NEC and Cabinet would be expected to adhere, therefore, would *not* be limited to those set out in the Manifesto. (Even if the Manifesto were made up of two separate documents, as has been suggested elsewhere — a popular version plus a longer, more detailed one — it would still not cover all of the work of a Government; and it would still progressively become out of date.) Both Government and NEC would, therefore, be expected always to refer to the basic Programme of the Party, as laid down by Conference.

The trade unions and joint control

How would the trade unions fit into this scheme for joint control? In truth, not very easily. Indeed, it is perhaps in the nature of the Party and the Movement that our process of policy-making will always remain an untidy business, never quite straightforward and logical.

The trade unions, for example, are partly inside the Party and partly outside it: their representatives sit on the NEC for example; but they also sit, with others, on the TUC General Council. As an integral part of the Party, they are involved in discussions on policy with a Labour Government; but they also negotiate *directly* with the Government, either alone or as part of the TUC. And so on. Not surprisingly, the temptation to play the Party off against the TUC, and vice versa, is one not easily resisted by the Parliamentary Leadership.

There are at least two possible approaches here. The first would be to accept completely the tri-partite nature of policy-making and implementation in the Labour Movement: that is, the process of joint control would have to be widened to include the TUC, along the lines of the existing TUC-Labour Party Liaison Committee.

In practice this would have to mean that the Party becomes a full partner in any negotiations between the Government and the TUC on matters which affect the policy of the Labour Party — including even such issues as pay policy and trade union law. The NEC and Party would gain, because it would mean an end to the business of 'concordats' being foisted upon the Party without even a trace of consultation. But the NEC could also find that it has lost some of its freedom of manoeuvre, having to accept a degree of responsibility for the success or failure of those jointly agreed policies.

The difficulty with this approach is that the TUC is a separate and distinct organisation, with its own Congress, its own policies, and its own long-term objectives. It is certainly not an organisation committed to a socialist transformation of society, or even to Labour's Programme; and, given the growth in membership of unions not affiliated to the Party, this is likely to become increasingly obvious in the years ahead.

An alternative approach would be to avoid involving the TUC directly in the procedures for joint control set out earlier. Instead, negotiations with the TUC would be conducted on the basis of policy positions jointly agreed, prior to these negotiations, between the NEC and the Parliamentary leadership. But this too would limit the NEC's freedom to distance itself from the Labour

Government of the day.

An end to "bourgeois democracy"?

It should not prove too difficult to draft the necessary constitutional and other amendments needed to establish joint control as the working practice of the Party in Government. After all, many other democratic socialist Parties (albeit some of them with a rather more compliant rank and file membership than ours) have taken such joint control very much for granted. Unlike ourselves however they have not tended to need to make detailed provisions for those in their constitutions. Instead they just practice it as a matter of course.

Our history is different. For it has been dominated by the dictates of "bourgeois democracy" — the term used, disparagingly, by Scandinavian social democrats to describe the British Labour Party's obsession with the rights of Members of Parliament and the sanctity of Cabinet Government. It is precisely because of this obsession, indeed, that elsewhere in this booklet we have included numerous other recommendations designed to tip the balance of power away from the Parliamentary wing and in favour of the Party. For all of these will help, in effect, to strengthen the authority of the NEC.

A SOCIALIST PLP: AN ALTERNATIVE TO JOINT CONTROL?

There could be, of course, a completely different route to achieving the implementation of Party policy — one that does not rely on enhancing the status and authority of the NEC on policy issues. This would be to rely on a combination of mandatory reselection, grass roots vigilance at constituency level, and the internal democratisation of the PLP, to provide the necessary pressure on Labour Cabinets, *via Members of Parliament*.

This approach cannot be dismised out of hand, especially if backed up, *inter alia*, by:

— open voting at PLP meetings (which would be the final authority on all matters concerning the work of the PLP — including on the whip).

70

- regular reports on the above, and on the record of the Labour Cabinet, to be circulated from Head Office to the CLPs.
- all principal front bench spokesmen to be elected, by *open* ballot.

There are, however, a number of serious objections to this approach.

First, it is not at all clear how Conference fits into the picture. Particular CLPs may, or may not, support particular Conference policies: there could, indeed, be a real danger of "Balkanisation" within the Party, and a serious loss of overall cohesion and sense of purpose.

Second, it is not all that easy in practice for a CLP to put the right kind of pressure on its MP — that is, to get him or her to combine with others in the PLP to put pressure on the Cabinet. MPs themselves, if they *do* respond to the views of their CLPs, will have to seek alliances with other MPs in order to get resolutions through the PLP; but they will have to bear in mind in doing so that to become a Minister, they will need to be elected by the PLP, or selected by the PM — a factor likely seriously to inhibit MPs from getting out of step with the PLP as a body.

Third, there is the role of the NEC. Does it, for example, retain its role as interpreter of Conference decisions? If so, will it have the right to bring its authority to bear on the Cabinet, or on the PLP? One possibility is that negotiations would have to become tri-partite, involving the Cabinet, the NEC and the PLP. If this were the case, the PLP would presumably have to be represented by either its officers or by its backbench representatives on the PLP Liaison Committee. But who is then representing who? For both the Cabinet and the PLP representatives would have been elected by the same body of people (unless, that is, the Cabinet is to be elected by Conference or an electoral college); whilst both the PLP and the NEC would presumably claim that *they* truly represent the views of the Party. In both cases, the basis of representation begins to get seriously confused.

And *fourth,* perhaps most important of all, we will be helping to strengthen both the "bourgeois myth" (the idea that the MP is responsible only to himself, to do the best he can for his constituency and his nation, subject only to the demands of his conscience) and the dominance over our political life or the

71

'Westminster ethos', which effectively and efficiently downgrades the importance of the extra-Parliamentary party.

In short, if we are serious about the Party outside Parliament having the right to insist on its policies being implemented, then we must use the extra-Parliamentary party's *own* instrument of authority, elected from itself. This instrument is the NEC.

2. Composition

Before looking at some specific proposals for changing the composition of the NEC, it might be helpful to set out some of the principles which might guide us in seeking reform:

1. *We need an executive body which is effectively accountable and answerable to the Party.* Democratic experience suggests that this can best be achieved by ensuring that the executive body — *as an executive* — is directly responsible to, and dismissible by, a sovereign democratic assembly. For the Party, we suggest, this implies that we should try to ensure that, as far as possible, the NEC is responsible directly to Conference, *and that it can be called directly to account* (e.g. any Conference, whether Annual Conference or a special one, should have the right to discuss the Executive or any of its officers). But this same principle would also tend to preclude the election of NEC members by bodies *other* than Party Conference, whether these be the PLP, or the YS, Local Government or Women's Conferences.

2. *The Executive should be fully representative of the membership of the Party, in the sense of being elected by the membership and answerable to it;* and each member should have a clear means of access and clear rights in this electoral process — implying, as far as our indirect, 'delegate democracy' is concerned, powers for members to mandate and instruct delegates at *every* level of the process. These considerations would tend to rule out entirely the possibility of representation being accorded to MPs *as* MPs ("representing" the PLP); or to councillors ("representing" Labour Groups), to Labour members on Area Health Authorities, or to Prospective Parliamentary Candidates ("representing" God knows who). For in cases such as these there can be no practical possibility of mandates from the membership: instead, we would be giving to certain members of the Party, who had been elected to perform certain tasks, special *extra* rights — and important rights at that — entirely denied to other members of the Party.

72

(It would be rather like giving extra voting rights, say, to an annual meeting of Political Education Officers, or to an annual meeting of CLP Treasurers; or indeed, it would be like giving to the NEC, as an NEC, a block vote all of its very own, at Conference). Representation, in short, must be from the basic building blocks of the Party — the CLPs and the trade unions.

3. *The Executive should reflect as accurately as practicable those political forces in the Party which provide its underlying strength and viability.* Only if it does so will decisions of the NEC either carry the necessary political clout, or be accepted as expressing the will and wishes of the Party (e.g. in interpreting the decisions of Conference). This points to the need to ensure that the 'two pillars' of the Party — the unions and the constituency parties — provide the fundamental basis for any system of representation (on the NEC and at Conference); and that this representation should be on a basis of *parity of representation* for the two pillars.

4. *The Executive should not exclude from its membership those best able to speak with authority on behalf of those sections of the Party, and those viewpoints in the Party, they are elected to represent.* The practical point here is not a positive one (in favour of elitism) but a negative one: namely the need to avoid making it impossible to recruit to the NEC the best, the most authoritive, the most experienced spokesmen who happen to be available — such as members of the TUC General Council (at present excluded) or Members of Parliament — on the doubtful grounds that such people cannot properly 'represent' rank and file. The latter approach merely confuses the issue: the real problem is not whether this or that individual is suitable, but how to ensure that he or she is fully answerable and accountable to his or her appropriate constituency in the Party.

5. *The Executive should reflect, as far as is practicable given the above considerations, the class, sex and ethnic make-up of the Party membership;* and our aim should be to ensure that the Party membership, in turn, reflects the make-up of the nation as a whole. This implies a measure of positive discrimination in our approach to composition — and especially as regards the very large proportion of the membership who are women.

6. *There should be a reasonable degree of continuity in membership on the Executive, so as to build up a body of*

experience and knowledge of the kind needed to enable it to effectively deal as an equal with a Labour Government. Again this need not imply any need to provide positively for incumbents to remain members for any length of time: but it does tend to rule out insisting on any kind of annual turnover, or some such, of membership.

7. *In suggesting changes to the composition of the NEC we should try, as far as we can, to build upon the existing structure, rather than go for wholesale reform.* The existing *political* make-up of the NEC does pretty accurately reflect the views of Conference and Party: and it would be unwise to propose changes so radical that the whole nature and complexion of the Executive was changed beyond recognition — not least because the changes would be strenuously resisted by many in both major wings of the Party.

The present position

The present composition of the NEC includes the following 29 members:

12 members, elected by the affiliated *trade unions,* at Conference.
7 members, elected by the *CLPs,* at Conference.
5 *women members,* elected by the whole Confeence.
1 *Treasurer,* elected by the whole Conference.
1 member, elected by the *co-op and socialist organisations.*
Leader and Deputy Leader, elected by the Parliamentary Labour Party.
1 member, elected by the *Young Socialist* Annual Conference.

A number of points are worth noting about the present composition:

1. No less than 18 out of the 29 are elected, in effect, by the trade unions (the trade unions control nearly 90 per cent of the votes). The 'election' procedure, for all of these posts, involves in practice a complex business of horse-trading between the major unions, with trade union delegates — at their delegate meeting — being advised by their trade union leaders on the outcome of this horse-trading. As a result, the bigger unions — and especially the union leaders engaged in the horse trading — are in a powerful position both to secure

places for their own representatives, and to 'blackball' those they wish to keep off.

2. Members of the TUC General Council are not eligible for nomination to the NEC (Standing Order 4 (3) d). This fact, combined with the heavy burden of work on senior trade union officials – and, too, given their own perception of the relative importance of the NEC and its activities – mean that able, senior trade union leaders seldom come on to the NEC – and certainly not for any length of time. Indeed, no less than five of the twelve in the trade union section are (or until the election were) MPs; and few if any of the remaining trade unionists play much of an active role in the activities of the NEC, apart from attendance at its 'statutory' committees.

3. No less than 21 out of the 29 members are, or were until the election, MPs (this includes all the members of the constituency and women's sections). For the constituency section, this is not surprising, given the difficulties involved in getting known; but it is much less 'understandable' in the eleven MPs elected, *de facto*, by the trade unions, except in terms of the points made in Point 2 above.

4. Only three of the 29 are not accountable, at least in some part, to Conference (Leader, Deputy Leader and YS representative); and even the Leader is now formally recognised in the constitution as being Leader of the whole Party. This does help to provide a healthy flavour, at Conference, of direct accountability by the NEC to delegates.

5. There are only seven women members of the NEC; and women fill only two out of the 24 places which are not reserved for women members.

2. *Proposals for Reform*

Since the renewed debate about the structure of the Party began, a number of proposals have been made for changing the composition of the NEC. We look at each of these, briefly, in the light of the principles outlined earlier.

i. *The balance between the CLPs and the unions*

The 1968 Report of the Committee of Enquiry included a proposal to abolish the five seats of the Women's Section, increasing the trade union section by three, and the constituency section by two. The proposal was not, however, endorsed by the NEC; nor was it put formally to Conference.[5] Nonetheless, the report itself *was* debated at the 1968 Conference: and it became clear during the debate that there was considerable support, even among the unions, for the principle of parity of representation on the NEC between the CLPs and the unions.

We believe that this should be taken as the starting point for any reform of the NEC — irrespective of any conclusions which may be reached about women's representation on the NEC or, indeed, representation at Conference itself: namely, that *we should aim for parity of 'direct' representation for the two major pillars of the Party — the CLPs and the unions.* (As we argue elsewhere, this would mirror the parity we also seek in representation and voting power between the unions and the CLPs at Conference.)

One anomaly which would still remain, of course, is the position of the *Treasurer,* since this post is elected by the whole Conference. However, once a proper balance in voting power between CLPs and unions has been achieved, election by the whole Conference could at last begin accurately to reflect the views of the Party as a whole.

ii. Abolition of the Women's Section?

The 1968 Report accepted that the women's section of the NEC, as it stands, is a complete anachronism. And it suggested that it would be a comparatively simple matter to transfer these five seats directly to the constituency section, thus providing a position quite close to parity with the unions.

But if we were to do this, there would be a real danger that the NEC would become almost completely male-dominated, since no women members have ever been elected from the trade union section, and only two have been able to make it, at any one time, in the constituency section. Moreover, we recognise only too clearly the very real problem facing women who seek to play an active political role in the Party. In our view, a substantial measure of positive discrimination is required; and this must certainly involve reserving a number of places on the Executive for women candidates.

The Group was divided, however, on how best to provide for this. One solution, favoured by some members of the Group,

76

involved retaining the existing women's section (five seats) but filling the seats by election from Women's Conference. Others, however, argued that there are a number of major difficulties with this approach:

i. It would mean more places on the Executive being filled by representatives not responsible or accountable in any real sense to Party Conference. Instead of enhancing the sense of direct answerability to Conference on the party of the NEC, this would reduce it. This, it was felt, would be a retrogade step.

ii. There is the degree to which Women's Conference is in practice representative of women in the Party. Certainly, at present, the basis of representation is not geared to provide an especially democratic forum. Unlike the Annual Conference of the Party the basis of voting is the same as that for representation (i.e. there are no block votes). Those entitled to attend are as follows:

   — *National Organisations* such as trade unions (if they have women members) can send up to twenty delegates.
   — *Women's Sections* can each send two.
   — *Women's Councils* (which, confusingly, themselves include representatives from the Women's Sections — plus women members of the YS, women members of Labour Groups, etc.) can also send two each.
   — *Constituency Parties,* where there are no womens organisation, can send two.

Clearly, this is a pattern of representation which makes little sense in democratic terms; it bears no relationship at all to the numbers of women members of the Party, or even of women members of the trade unions. But then Women's Conference *is* only an advisory Conference; and the fairly relaxed basis of representation reflects this. To use it as a basis for representation to the NEC would thus entail the wholesale revision of its representative base — possibly thereby undermining much of its value as a sounding board for the views of Labour Women.

iii. There is the simple democratic objection that women members in the Party — to the extent that Women's Conference *was* reformed to represent more accurately their views — would have two votes compared to the one for male members. Similarly, women members would have the right — via the appropriate machinery — to call to account those members of the NEC elected by their own Conference — a right entirely denied to male members. At the same time, however, women members *would* still have the right to vote for, and call to account, the 'ordinary' members (men or women) of the constituency section.

Reserved Seats?

An alternative would be *to reserve a certain number of seats in each of the two main (equal) sections for women candidates*. In order to overcome any resistance on the part of the unions to having some of the existing representatives *replaced* by women, the number of representatives in each of the main sections should be increased; and it would also be appropriate to keep to the principle of parity between the two wings of the Party, and provide the same number of 'reserved' seats in each.

Thus a suitable arrangement might be to include three 'reserved' seats in each section (trade unions and constituencies) — thus increasing the effective "Women's Section" by one; whilst increasing the two main sections to 15 each to ensure that none of the men in the trade union section need to give up their places to make way for women members. Thus, for the first time, the NEC would include *women* representatives from the trade union section; and the overall chances for women would also be improved because potential NEC members would be likely to enter the lists of the *general* CLP section much more strongly than in the past.

Trade Union Representation

It was noted earlier that members of the General Council of the TUC are not allowed to be members of the NEC (the two bodies actually meet on the same morning of the same day each month). There seems to be no good reason why this state of affairs should continue — especially in view of the way in which the Party and the TUC now accept the need to march in step. We propose, therefore, that this provision in the rules be removed.

A much more important issue, however, concerns the democratic processes leading up to the election of the trade union representatives themselves. Clearly, this is a far wider issue than merely the election of the NEC; the Group believe that the Party does need to bring this issue out into the open and discuss the procedures the trade unions as they bear upon the activities of the Party.

It is worth noting, however, some of the severe problems involved in trying to reform trade union procedures as they effect the election of the NEC. In the first place, precisely because the unions are affiliated at *national* level, there are no exact counterparts — on the union side of the Party — to the local parties. We cannot, therefore, easily devise a system for nominations to come up directly from the trade union "grass roots": instead, we *have* to think in terms of using either the trade union conferences, their executives, or their Party Conference delegations. And since many of our unions do not have an *annual* conference, it is likely that the Party would continue to have to leave the decisions either to the union executives or to their delegations to Party Conference, to be taken in the light of their own conference policies.

With either system the horse-trading on NEC places will continue — unless, that is, we are willing to insist that the block votes of the unions are cast on the basis of being proportional to the level of support for each candidate within the delegations themselves. We do not rule this out as a possibility: and it may be something the Party needs to discuss when considering the broader issues of the block vote.

iii. Representation from Local Government

One proposal that is likely to receive serious consideration by the Enquiry is the inclusion on the NEC of representation "from local government". The 'constituency' usually proposed in this context is the Local Government Conference; but it would presumably be possible to create alternative procedures — for example, the appointment of one or all of the three leaders of the Labour Groups on the local government associations (AMA, ACC and ADC) or election through a ballot of Labour councillors.

Whichever procedure is preferred, however, they all suffer from the same crucially important defect in terms of democratic procedures: namely that, as noted earlier, it would mean creating a specially privileged position for a handful of Labour Party members — giving them significant extra rights to ordinary members merely because they had been chosen by the Party to carry out certain duties as elected representatives. The chosen NEC members would not be representatives from the basic building blocks of the Party. They would be representatives of a group who are already representatives.

Election from Local Government Conference?

The proposal for representation from the Local Government Conference is marked by a further deep flaw. For the Conference itself is simply not constituted as a democratic body able to take decisions or to elect representatives in any democratic manner.

Representation to the Conference at present includes the following.[6]

A maximum of 5 representatives

Greater London Council Labour Group
Inner London Education Authority Labour Group
Metropolitan County Labour Groups
Non-Metropolitan County Labour Groups
Welsh County Labour Groups
Scottish Regional Labour Groups
London Borough Labour Groups
Metropolitan District Labour Groups

A maximum of 4 representatives

Non-Metropolitan District Labour Groups
Welsh District Labour Groups
Scottish District Labour Groups
Regional Councils of the Labour Party
County Labour Parties (Regional in Scotland)
District Labour Parties
London Local Government Committees

A maximum of 2 representatives

Labour Groups in Party, Community and Town Councils

This pattern of representation accurately reflects the *nature* of the Conference. For it was never designed to take decisions:

it is, rather, an informal discussion forum, organised into subject groups, where councillors can exchange information and experience, question and argue with Ministers (or Shadow Spokesmen) and convey their views to the NEC and to the Parliamentary Leadership. (Admittedly these are plenary sessions: but again, the object is merely to exchange views and to air grievancies.) There are no votes. And there are no procedures for taking them, apart from a rough and ready show of hands by those present. What is more, were the Party foolish enough to change the whole basis of representation to this Conference — merely in order to provide a method of providing representation on the NEC — the Conference would probably lose a good deal of its value and usefulness to the Party: and the 'local government interest' in the Party, far from being strengthened, could actually be weakened.

The call for local government representation is, of course, mainly motivated by a wish to change the political complexion of the NEC. But there is, in addition, a serious concern among Labour councillors over what they see as the inability of the NEC to appreciate properly the problems of local government. And there *is* a need to respond to this. Certainly the NEC must ensure that there is adequate representation for councillors on its various policy (advisory) sub-committees. (In addition, that is, to that on the existing Regional and Local Government Sub-Committee, which has very substantial representation indeed from local government.) The NEC must also ensure that the new consultation procedures it has agreed include as much participation as possible on the part of Labour Councillors. But should we go further than this?

We could, for example, allow an observer from local government — chosen say, jointly by the Labour groups on the AMA, the ACC, and ADC — to attend the NEC, in the same way that an observer now attends from the PLP (the Chief Whip) and from the Labour Group in the European Parliament. (In practice, given the very divergent interests of the three different kinds of local authorities, we might have to allow three local government observers, one from each: but this would not present any special problems.) Alternatively, we could provide for a "reserved place" in the constituency section of the NEC — as suggested earlier for women — which could only be filled by a sitting councillor.

But this latter suggestion would obviously create a dangerous precedent — for we could then find it difficult to resist providing similar reserved places not only for the PLP but also for the Labour Group in the European Parliament (and for Labour representatives in Area Health Authorities, on the Consumer Councils of the Nationalised Industry, etc., etc.).

We suggest, therefore, that a place be created for *one* observer at the NEC, to be selected by the Labour Groups of the AMA, ACC and ADC. (An election by ballot of Labour councillors could serve to exaggerate the importance of the position.)

iv. Regional Councils

A further proposal likely to be taken seriously by the Enquiry is for representation from the eleven Regional Councils. (Both APEX and the GMWU are pushing this.) It is not at all clear, however, what advantages are expected to accrue from this. In the context of a complete shift to a regionally-based federal structure for the Party (that is, with resolutions to Annual Conference being composited and debated first at regional level, etc.) this proposal may make some sense.

But why on earth should the Party *want* to fragment itself in this way? In what way would it help policy formation, say on economic policy, if decisions are taken first at regional level? Would the regions then vote at Conference region by region? If so, how will this improve accountability? If not, what is the point of the earlier regional decisions? And so on. Yet unless these issues are all sorted out, and a clear case made out for this complete change in the nature of the Party, the proposal for regional representation to the NEC does not really begin to stand up.

Three further points could be made here:

First, the basis of representation to the Regional councils is little different to that for Annual Conference — that is, the Councils are completely dominated by the trade union vote.[7] As presently constituted, therefore, all of the representatives from the eleven regions (assuming one from each, as proposed in Diane Hayter's Fabian Pamphlet) are likely to be from the trade unions, thus making it even more difficult to establish either parity between CLPs and unions or for the adequate provision for the representation of women.

Second, a reform to provide regional representation would introduce yet a further tier in an already complex chain of representation, thus further widening the gap between the NEC and the membership. *Our* aim, on the contrary is to strengthen accountability.

Third, it would remove from a large section of the NEC — at least a third of its members in all — any element whatsoever of accountability to Annual Conference.

v. *"Rank and File" representation*

Partly as a reaction to the large number of MPs elected the NEC (21 out of 29, just previous to the General Election, at which three of them lost their Parliamentary seats) proposals have been made to provide a section of the NEC reserved for the "rank and file". It is not clear, however, how wide the *exclusions* should go: it would certainly exclude MPs, and presumably members of the Lords — but it could also exclude, presumably, councillors, trade union officials and anyone else with a 'position' in the Labour Movement.

There are at least two possibilities:

i. We could provide a couple of 'reserved' seats in the enlarged CLP section, in the same way as that proposed above for women.

ii. We could provide a new section on the NEC for these members. This could, of course, upset the position of parity between the CLPs and the unions — unless, that is, we were to increase the members of trade unionists to restore the position. (But the NEC would then be heading for a total membership of 40.)

On balance, we would prefer the first option, were the call for this kind of representation to be sustained. *The majority of the Group believe, however, that there is no real case for this kind of representation.* The need is to ensure that *whoever* is elected to the NEC is made fully accountable to the Party.

vi. *The PLP*

The objections to giving MPs representation direct from the PLP itself have already been indicated earlier, since the democratic case against such a change applies equally to Labour Groups and to the Labour Group in the European Assembly. But is there a case for providing a reserved seat (or seats), within the CLP section, for MPs?

We do not think so. The fact is that there are already two seats reserved *de facto* for MPs (the Leader and Deputy Leader); the Chief Whip already attends as an observer (and in practice is given full rights to speak "on behalf of" the PLP); and MPs are likely, for the foreseeable future, to retain a considerable presence on the NEC. We do not believe, however, that it would make more sense for the PLP to be represented by an observer more able to speak on behalf of the whole PLP, rather than — as in the case of the Chief Whip — only on behalf of the Parliamentary Leadership. *We suggest, therefore, that the Chairman of the PLP replaces the Chief Whip as an observer to the NEC.*

vii. Young Socialists

In the light of the criteria set out at the beginning of this paper the position of the YS representative (elected by the YS Conference) does appear to be anomalous. Admittedly, it seems reasonable enough on the face of it to provide a slot on the NEC for someone able to articulate the views and aspirations of young Party members. On the other hand, there seems to be no particular reason why the objections raised earlier should not apply with equal force to the YS Conference. For if we believe that NEC members should be accountable, as directly as possible, to the membership of the Party; that the best way to do this is to make the Executive directly responsible to the "Parliament of the Party"; and that the basis of representation should be built up, as far as possible, equally upon the 'two pillars' of the Party (unions and CLPs) then there is a case for ending the present arrangement and replacing it by direct election from Annual Conference. This could be done by providing another 'reserved seat' for a YS member for election by the whole Conference (as with the Treasurer).

Other members of the Group, however, pointed to the need to give as much weight as possible within the Party to the democratic 'self-government' of the YS: and that we should not seek to make changes in the composition of the NEC unless the reasons for doing so were extremely compelling. No conclusion was reached by the Group on this issue.

viii. Leader and Deputy Leader

We have set out, in a separate chapter, our pro
the Leader and Deputy Leader. These posts
carry with them ex officio representation on th

ix. Socialist and Co-operative Organisations

Although we have a number of serious reservations concerning
the democratic basis of filling this position — and indeed, reservations about the continuance of the position itself — we are
unable at this point to come forward with firm proposals.

Footnotes

1. To succeed, indeed, it would involve *inter alia* ending the provision for
   independent trade unions to affiliate nationally to the Party, in favour
   of direct membership at branch or constituency level.
2. Neither local authority Labour Groups (nor the Labour Group in the
   European Assembly) pose problems of the same degree for the Party.
3. One issue left open here, and taken up later, is the role of the TUC in
   all this.
4. The Norwegian Social Democrats operate a procedure rather similar to
   this, when in Government, except that their pre-Cabinet liaison committee includes representatives from the Norwegian equivalent of our
   TUC.
5. After kicking the matter about for some four years the NEC decided, in
   1972, not to support any change to the Women's Section.
6. Representatives from Labour Groups must be elected members of their
   authority; representatives from Regional Councils of the Labour Party
   must be members of their Regional Council Executive Committee;
   representatives from County (Regional in Scotland) and District Labour
   Parties must be members of the management committees appointing
   them; representatives from London Local Government Committees
   must be members of the Local Government Committee appointing
   them.
7. One difference from Conference on the basis of representation to
   Regional Councils is that such bodies as County and District Labour
   Parties, County Associations of Trade Councils, and Women's Councils
   each have one vote. (CLPs and trade unions have one vote per 1,000
   members.)

.. We are of course in favour of the proposition that a Labour Government should regularly and seriously consult the trade unions and the Labour Party, before taking major decisions.

2. The purpose of this note is to give the reasons for our fundamental objections to the proposal for "Joint Control" set out in the Background Paper on the NEC.

3. "Joint Control" envisages a joint Cabinet-NEC Government and leadership in which each side would have a veto over any action of the other.

4. The proposal is based on the assumption of a basic uniformity of interest and purpose between the PLP, the NEC and the mass organisations of the Party. It puts its faith in the mere institutionalising of consultation between leaders with a sanction that could only lead to stalemate.

5. The Labour Party structure reflects the class structure of our society. For a complex of reasons the majority of the PLP today either support or are unable to resist establishment values and establishment policies. For the foreseeable future the PLP is likely to remain the conservative wing of the Labour movement. Conference on the other hand, despite the undue deference of some trade unionists to the Parliamentary leadership, does over a period adopt policies that represent the interests of the working people. This basic conflict cannot be resolved by better communication between leaders. It can only be resolved over a period by making the PLP as a whole genuinely responsible to Conference and each MP genuinely accountable to his local Party and clearly responsible for carrying out Party policy.

6. The proposal embodies a fatal confusion of identities and responsibility between the two bodies. The Party's role is to make policy, select candidates, consider at Conference the performance of its representatives and to bear the brunt of political struggle outside Parliament. The role of the Parliamentary Party is to implement policy. The NEC between Conferences are responsible for exerting the maximum pressure possible on the Parliamentary leadership to carry out Con-

ference policies in full: it is not their job to do deals with the Parliamentary leadership which they later must justify to Conference.

7. The clear independence of the NEC is vital if they are to be effective in performing this role, and accountable to the Conference for doing so. "Joint Control" would mean the giving up of this independence, the increased separation of the NEC from the rank and file and the tendency for them to be absorbed into the world of the Parliamentary leadership.

8. We have very clear experience of what happens in these situations. During the lifetime of the last Labour Government, the TUC, its bureaucracy and some trade union leaderships were extensively and, indeed, assiduously consulted by the Prime Minister and the Chancellor of the Exchequer on policy. As a result, much of the trade union leadership and trade union officials found themselves trapped into trying to deliver rank and file support for policies of wage restraint masquerading as incomes policies, rather than representing their own rank and file opposition to such policies. The Government having secured the support of trade union leaders for its "incomes policies", ignored trade union opposition to public expenditure cuts. This damaging situation persisted until rank and file pressure forced trade union leaders to withdraw their support shortly before the last General Election.

9. We can scarcely advocate that we change the rules of the Party in order to ensure the repetition of this process extended to the NEC as well as the TUC.

Vladimir Derer
Frances Morrell
Reg Race
Peter Willsman